In the Footsteps of Jack the Ripper

J. P. Sperati

Edited by Louise Cissel

All correspondence for
In the Footsteps of Jack the Ripper
should be addressed to:

Irregular Special Press
Endeavour House
170 Woodland Road
Sawston
Cambridge
CB22 3DX

*****

Copyright © 2021 Baker Street Studios Limited
All rights reserved
Typesetting is in Times New Roman font

ISBN: 978-1-901091-78-6

Proof reading & editing: Louise Cissel
Front cover picture: Shutterstock
Footprints icon: Created by Giuditta Valentina Gentile
from Noun Project

*****

All rights reserved. No part of this publication may be reproduced, stored in a retrieval system, or transmitted, in any form or by any means, electronic, mechanical, photocopying, recording or otherwise, without the prior permission of the Irregular Special Press.

*****

Every effort has been made to ensure accuracy, but the publishers do not hold themselves responsible for any consequences that may arise from errors or omissions. Whilst the contents are believed to be correct at the time of going to press, changes may have occurred since that time or will occur during the currency of this publication.

For the EWB

Contents

Backdrop to the Whitechapel Murders of 1888 7
The Canonical Five Jack the Ripper Murders 15
   Mary Ann 'Polly' Nichols (Friday 31st August 1888) 15
      Whitechapel Road 20
   Annie Chapman (Saturday 8th September 1888) 21
      Hanbury Street 28
   Elizabeth Stride (Sunday 30th September 1888) 29
      The *Princess Alice* Disaster 33
   Catherine Eddowes (Sunday 30th September 1888) 34
      Hopping 42
      Model Dwellings 42
   Mary Kelly (Friday 9th November 1888) 44
      Spitalfields 52
      Coroner's Court 54

The Genesis of Jack the Ripper? 57
   Annie Millwood (Saturday 25th February 1888) 57
      White's Row 58
   Ada Wilson (Wednesday 28th March 1888) 58
      Bow 60
   Emma Elizabeth Smith (Tuesday 3rd April 1888) 62
      Brick Lane 64
   Martha Tabram (Tuesday 7th August 1888) 65
      George Yard Buildings and Toynbee Hall 69

The Return of Jack the Ripper? 73
   Catherine Mylett (Thursday 20th December 1888) 73
      Poplar 75
   Alice McKenzie (Wednesday 17th July 1889) 76
      Castle Alley 78
   The Pinchin Street Torso (Tuesday 10th September 1889) 79
      Pinchin Street 82
   Frances Coles (Friday 13th November 1891) 83
      Swallow Gardens 86

Clues and Red Herrings 89

Suspects Assemble 93
   Joseph Barnett 93
   Dr. Neill Cream 94
   Montague Druitt 95

Sir William Withey Gull 95
Aaron Kosminski 96
James Maybrick 97
Michael Ostrog 97
Dr. Alexander Pedachenko 98
Walter Sickert 98
Dr. Stanley 99
Dr. Francis Tumblety 99
Prince Albert Christian Edward Victor 100

A Singular Theory **101**

A Final Thought **121**

Jack the Ripper Walks **123**
The Canonical Five Walk 123
The Grand Tour 154

References & Acknowledgements **183**

Indexes **185**
General Index 185
Persons Index 189
Places Index 196
Streets Index 203

BACKDROP TO THE WHITECHAPEL MURDERS OF 1888

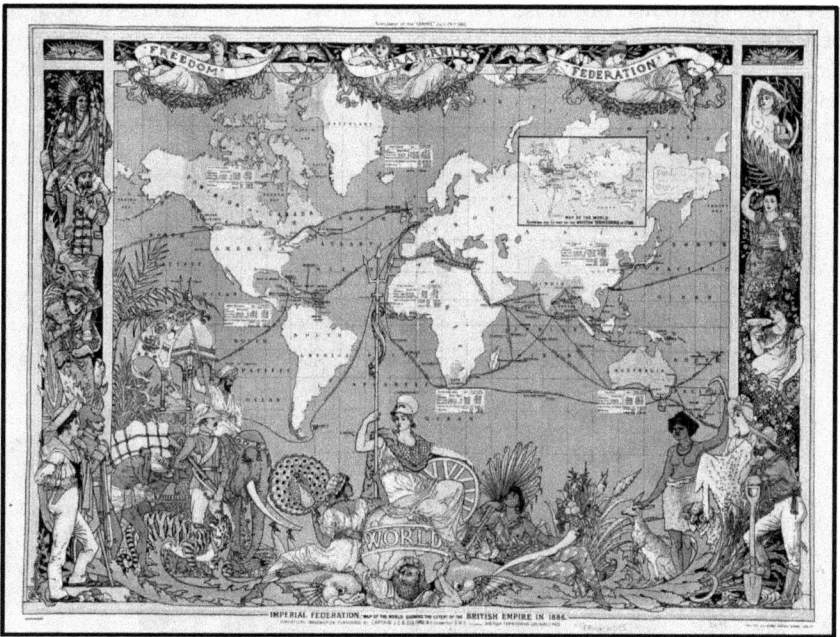

[World map dating from 1886 with shaded countries
being those that formed the British Empire]

By 1888 London was the centre of the greatest empire ever known, an empire that the Victorians would like to think was based on trade, justice, language, and culture. Queen Victoria had been on the thrown for over half a century and there was stability within her domains. The British Empire ruled a quarter of the world (13.7 million square miles) with English being spoken by around 40% of the world's population of 1.5 billion persons. There were dominions, colonies and protectorates all of which were ultimately administered from London. It was true to say that what Britain did not already have in its grasp it did not want. London was the largest jewel in the imperial crown, and the West End was a place of opulence, light, the arts, and the latest technology. As Dr. Samuel Johnson put it to James Boswell: 'Why, Sir, you find no man, at all intellectual, who is willing to leave London. No, Sir, when a man is tired of London, he is tired of life; for there is in London all that life can afford'.

However, beneath this golden veneer of respectability there was another story to be told. As an empire built ostensibly on trade, the port and manufacturing cities of Birmingham, Manchester, Bristol, Newcastle, Liverpool and the like played a large part in its creation. They attracted peoples from every part of the globe, and London being the largest was the world's central exchange. It was a cosmopolitan city unlike any other, but those coming were often poor, or refugees looking for new prospects, or those not particularly welcome. Dr. Watson, in *A Study in Scarlet*, expressed it perfectly when he wrote, 'under such circumstances I naturally gravitated to London, that great cesspool into which all the loungers and idlers of the Empire are irresistibly drained'.

[Immigrants arriving in London at the turn of the 20th century]

Backdrop to the Whitechapel Murders of 1888

For London it was not the West End that was the problem, but the East End where the docks were located, and where the poor worked and lived among the influx of foreign peoples who arrived on ships from which they could not afford to travel far. This part of the metropolis offered poverty, squalor, darkness, overcrowding, homelessness, and starvation.

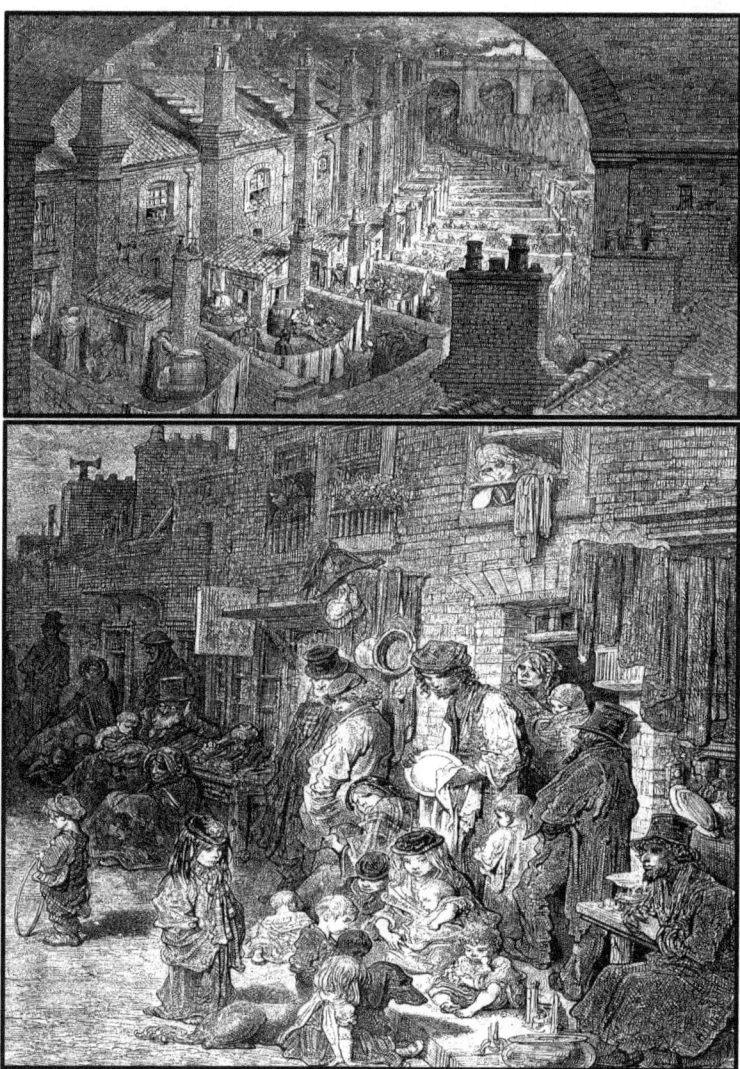

[*Over London by Rail* (top) and *Wentworth Street, Whitechapel* (bottom) – 1869 images by Gustave Doré of the East End]

The sketches of Gustave Doré made in 1869, and published in 1872 as a set of 180 engravings under the title *London: A Pilgrimage*, give a good indication of what the East End was like. Doré and journalist Blanchard Jerrold joined forces spending many days and nights exploring fashionable London, as well as the night refuges, common lodging houses, and opium dens of the East End. Both men were shocked by what they discovered, and although there was criticism that only extremes were illustrated, and that there were already changes being made to better the lot of the poor, those drawings do remain an indication of the backdrop against which Jack the Ripper operated.

[Victorian photographs of the conditions that prevailed in the East End]

Backdrop to the Whitechapel Murders of 1888

[More evidence of the squalor that was the East End]

Around 900,000 persons lived in the East End and of those around a quarter were in Whitechapel itself. They lived in common lodging houses, and overcrowded slums made up of courts and alleyways where more than one family might occupy a single room – many lived on the streets and most sought solace in the public houses. Infant mortality was also around a quarter.

[Inside a common lodging house in Spitalfields. Such establishments were often the haunt of criminals and prostitutes. The Common Lodging Houses Acts of 1851 and 1853 required the residents to vacate the premises between 10 a.m. and late afternoon – most just walked the streets]

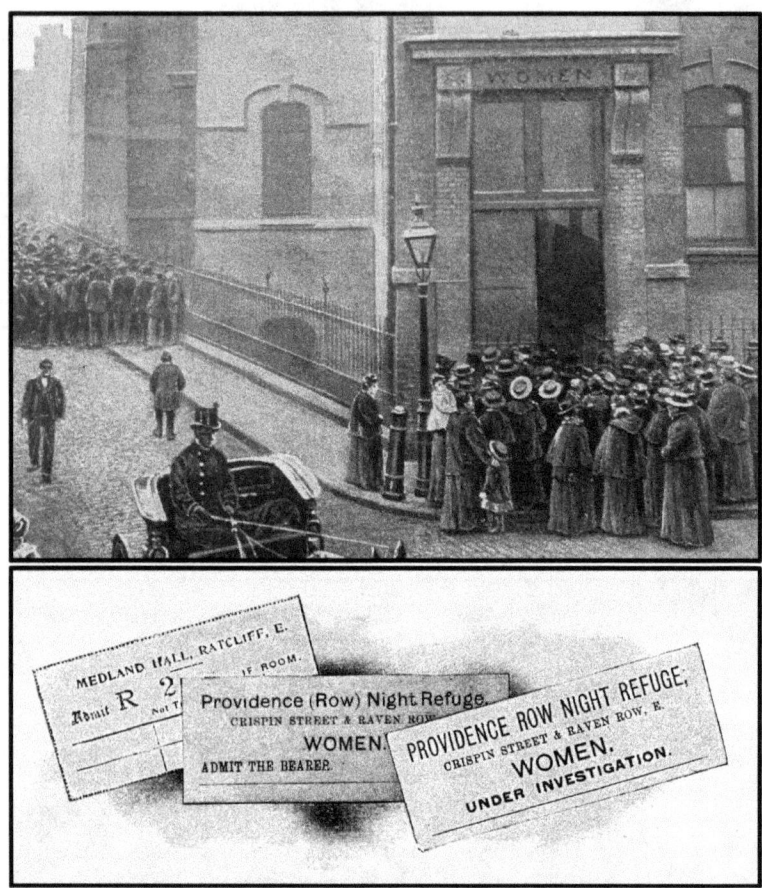

[Queuing outside Providence Row night refuge in Crispin Street – note the separate entrances for men and women (top). Those lucky enough to gain entry would be given an admission ticket for the night (bottom)]

Work was intermittent with the docks employing people on a day-by-day basis as was required. There were other employers but in all cases wages were low (£1-£2 a week and falling) and the hours long (up to 20 hours a day). Children and women were expected to work when they could, and the latter would be 'encouraged' to become part-time prostitutes to supplement a family's income – most were chronic alcoholics. In Whitechapel alone there were estimated to be 5,000 (out of 80,000 for the whole of London) prostitutes. The going rate for a young attractive woman was between half-a-crown and 10 shillings, but considerably lower otherwise. Alcohol in the form of gin was widely available and cheap. A common advertising slogan of the time was 'Drunk for a penny, dead drunk for tuppence'.

Another problem was the influx of some 50,000 Jewish persons from Russia, Poland, and Germany (many unable to speak or read English). As the 1880s were a time of recession (part of what was termed the 'Long Depression' between 1873 and 1896) any work was at a premium, so it is perhaps not surprising that this group of people were to become vilified for stealing English jobs and adding to the social problems that already existed.

[Daily queues would form of those eager for work]

Given the circumstances at the time it could be argued that it is surprising that there was not, as a percentage of population, even more crime than there was in the East End. Sherlock Holmes would agree that proportionally there was less crime in cities for as he put it in *The Adventure of the Copper Beeches*, 'It is my belief, Watson, founded upon my experience, that the lowest and vilest alleys in London do not present a more dreadful record of sin than does the smiling and beautiful countryside'. This was to change in the autumn of 1888 …

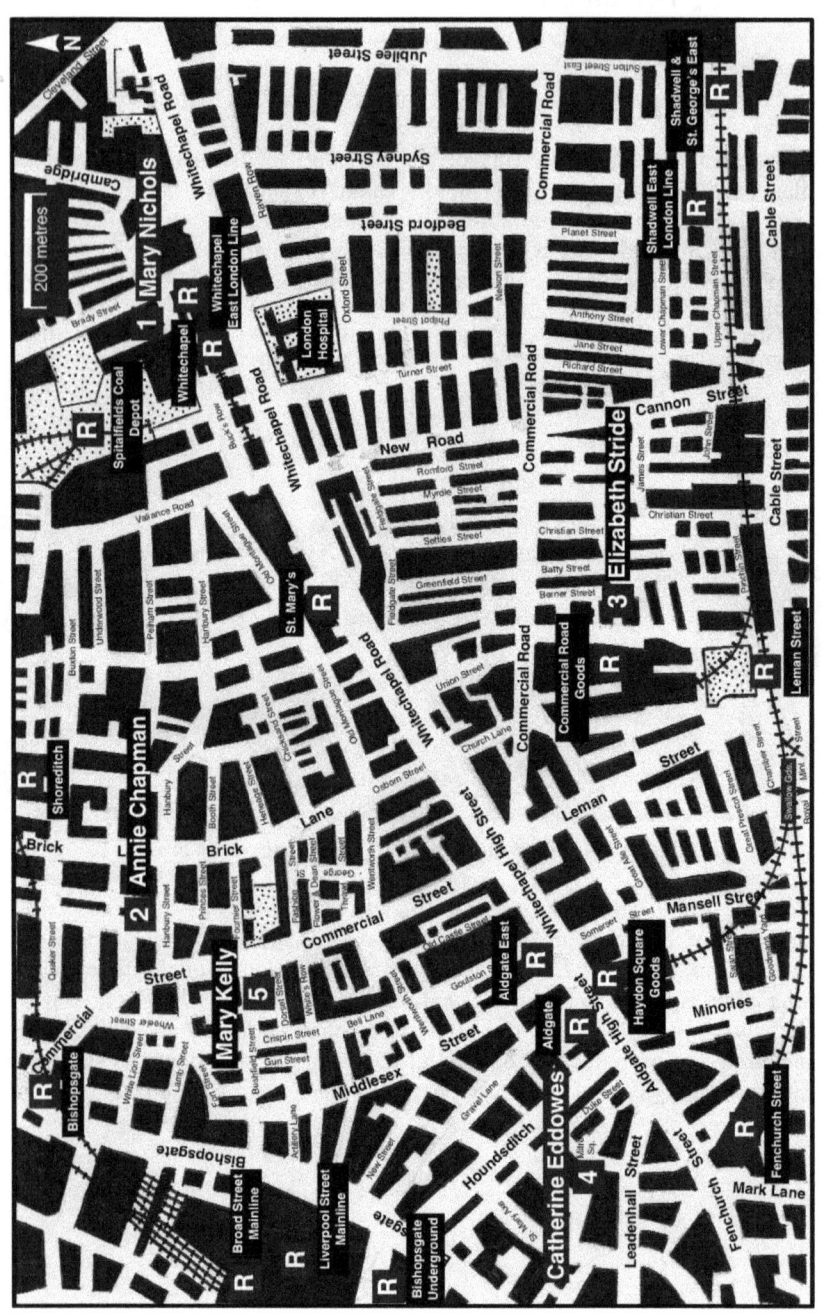

[1888 street map of the Canonical 5 Jack the Ripper Murders]

THE CANONICAL FIVE JACK THE RIPPER MURDERS

There is no particular agreement among historians, the police, or the 'Ripperlogists' as to just how many murders can be attributed to Jack the Ripper since one of the many dangers of being a female prostitute in the East End at that time was violent death. However, it is generally agreed that there were at least 5 victims, these being known as the canonical 5, and it is these that will be considered first.

MARY ANN 'POLLY' NICHOLS (FRIDAY 31ST AUGUST 1888)

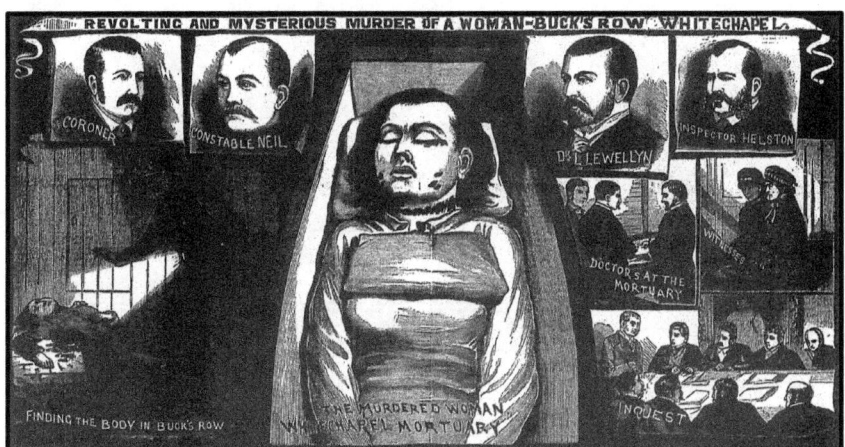

[*The Illustrated Police News* drawings of the Mary Nichols murder]

For Police Constable John Neil it started as a night on the beat like any other, but at around 3.45 a.m. he came across the body of a woman lying on the pavement close to a stable-yard in connection with Essex Wharf in Buck's Row (now Durward Street) which runs parallel with the railway line close to Whitechapel Underground station opened in 1876. At first, and because the street had only a single light at the eastern end, he assumed that the woman had fallen down drunk and was merely sleeping off the effects of her drinking. However, closer inspection revealed that her face was stained with blood and that her throat had been cut from ear-to-ear.

In fact, Neil was not the first to see the body, for only a few minutes earlier Charles Cross, a horse-cart driver on his way to work, had passed the same spot, as had Robert Paul, another horse-cart driver. They had both noted that the woman was on her back with her skirt raised almost to her abdomen, but failed to see that her throat had been cut and thought that she might just be dead drunk. They pulled her skirt back down and went on their way to work vowing to tell the first policeman they came across, which as it happened was Police Constable Jonas Mizen who they found on patrol in Hanbury Street (see page 28).

[Buck's Row in Victorian times (top left), the gated stable entrance where Police Constable Neil found the body of Mary Nichols (top right), as reported in the press (bottom left), and the same spot in 2021 – the stable entrance being by the Durward Street exit to Whitechapel station with the former Buck's Row Board School, now Trinity Hall residential flats, in the background (bottom right)]

The Canonical Five Jack the Ripper Murders

[A police ambulance was a practical, albeit crude, method for transporting bodies to the mortuary]

Neil was joined by another officer, Police Constable John Thain who had passed Buck's Row at 3.30 a.m. and he verified that he had seen nobody at that time. Thain went to fetch local doctor, Rees Llewellyn. Mizen then arrived and was sent to collect an ambulance (which in those days was merely a trolley on which the body could be transported to the nearest mortuary). While waiting Neil made enquiries at properties in the immediate area, but nobody had heard or seen anything.

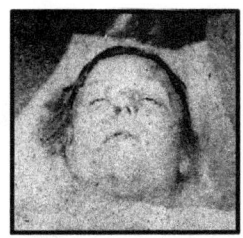

[Mortuary photograph of Mary Nichols]

It was only when examined at the mortuary that the full extent of the injuries became known. In addition to almost severing the head, the abdomen had been ripped up, and the bowels were protruding. The abdominal wall, the whole length of the body, had been cut open, and on either side were two incised wounds almost as severe as the centre one. They reached from the lower part of the abdomen to the breast-bone.

A local newspaper wrote that Dr Llewellyn had said that, 'she was ripped open just as you see a dead calf at the butcher's'. Even so these injuries were not as severe as those inflicted on later Jack the Ripper victims, which has led many to conclude that the killer was interrupted. It was also reported that the wounds had been inflicted by a left-handed person – a statement that Dr. Llewellyn was to later retract. Incredibly, up to that point, it was thought possible that the victim had committed suicide by cutting her own throat.

The next step was the identification of the body. The victim was 5 feet 2 inches tall, had a small scar on her forehead, 3 missing teeth (some reports claim 5), brown hair that was turning grey, a dark complexion, and was middle-aged. Her possessions amounted to just a comb, a broken fragment of a mirror, and a white handkerchief. Her clothes included a reddish-brown Ulster coat, a newish brown linsey frock, 2 petticoats (with the mark of the Lambeth Workhouse in Prince's Road), a pair of men's boots and a new black straw bonnet trimmed with black velvet. It was not long before she was identified as being Mary Ann 'Polly' Nichols of No. 18 Thrawl Street (a common lodging house). She had an estranged husband, William Nichols, whom she had married in 1864 and by whom she had had 5 children. He was able to add that she was actually 43-years old.

[The Frying Pan public house today]

Polly's movements prior to her murder are well documented. It had been cold for the time of year, and raining frequently with some thunder and lightning. At 11.00 p.m. she had been seen walking (probably soliciting) in the Whitechapel Road and at around 12.30 a.m. she was spotted leaving the Frying Pan public house on the corner of Brick Lane and Thrawl Street. Polly was on her way back to the lodging house where around an hour later she was thrown out for not having the 4d. fee for the night.

Her last known appearance was in Osborn Street, where at the corner with Whitechapel Road, she met Emily Holland (a friend, fellow prostitute, and roommate) with whom she spoke with for around 8 minutes. She told Emily that she had had her lodging money 3 times over that day but had spent it on drink – she appeared very drunk and staggered against a wall – but added that with her new bonnet she would have no trouble in finding a client and her doss money.

[The junction of Osborn Street and Whitechapel Road where Mary Nichols met Emily Holland as photographed in Victorian times (top) and in 2020 (bottom)]

The prevalent theories were that Polly was murdered by a gang, a seaman, or a slaughterman/butcher. The police did their job diligently searching over 200 doss/common lodging houses and made 14 arrests, but all to no avail. On the 6th September Mary was buried at Manor Park Cemetery, Forest Gate. All would have been forgotten if there had not been another similar murder under 2 days later …

WHITECHAPEL ROAD

[The London Hospital in Whitechapel Road, circa 1900]

Whitechapel Road takes its name from the 14th century white chapel which stood at the east end of the road. The Whitechapel Bell Foundry and the London Hospital are both located here.

[King George V at the Whitechapel Bell Foundry inspecting the 'Victory' bell for Westminster Abbey in 1919]

The bell foundry was established in 1420 in Houndsditch, but moved to Whitechapel Road in 1738, taking over the grounds and buildings of the Artichoke Inn. Many of the world's great bells have been cast here, including those for Westminster Abbey, Big Ben, and America's original Liberty Bell.

The London Hospital was founded in 1740 near Moorfields, but in 1753 moved to its present location in Whitechapel Road. The hospital, designed by Boulton Mainwaring, was finished in 1757 and for its time was the finest hospital building in London. East and West Wings were added in 1775 and 1778 respectively. The Medical College was founded in 1783 by Sir William Blizard (who performed operations until the age of 84, and was instrumental in founding the Royal College of Surgeons) and Thomas Maddocks. One of the medical students in 1866 was Dr. Thomas John Barnardo, who later founded the Dr. Barnardo's Homes for children. The Medical College became part of the University of London in 1948, and in 1990 the hospital became the home of the hospital's Helicopter Emergency Medical Service (the first in the United Kingdom). Inside the main entrance hall are a bell from the nearby Whitechapel Bell Foundry and a plaque to Thomas Lester (who built the foundry in 1738).

ANNIE CHAPMAN (SATURDAY 8TH SEPTEMBER 1888)

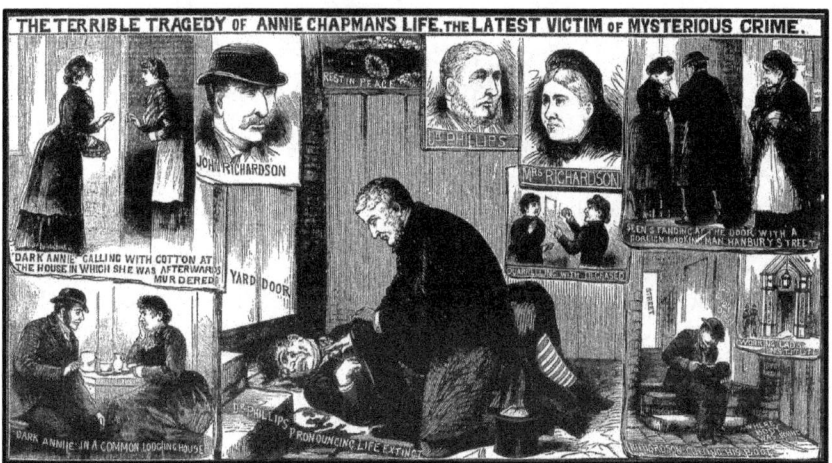

[Coverage of the Annie Chapman murder in *The Illustrated Police News*]

The second Jack the Ripper body was to be found in the back yard of No. 29 Hanbury Street. The victim was another prostitute (and also a sieve-maker, who in addition earned money from crochet work, making antimacassars, and selling flowers) by the name of Annie Chapman, though also known as Annie Siffey, Annie Sivvy, and 'Dark Annie'.

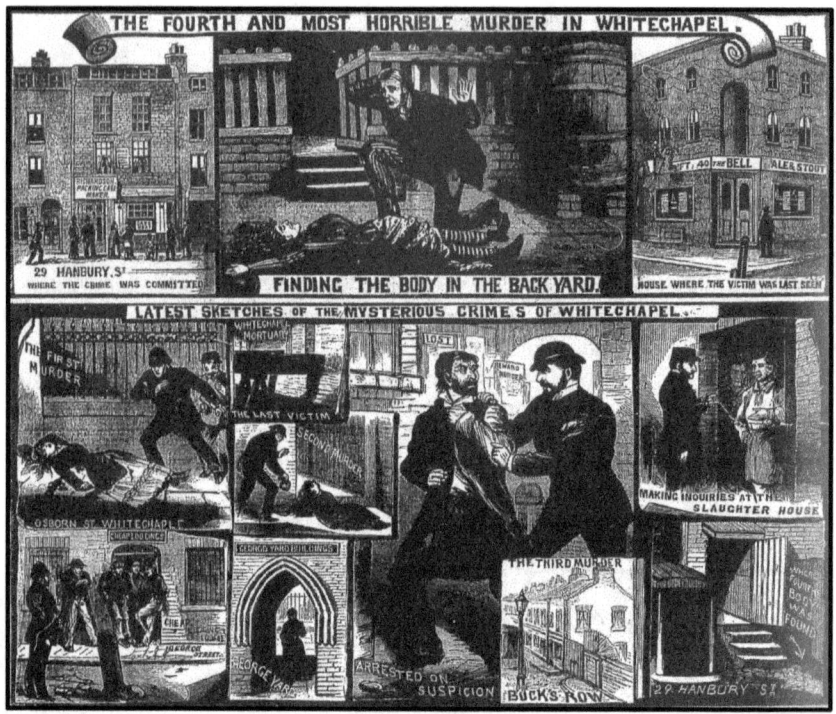

[Further coverage of the Annie Chapman murder in *The Illustrated Police News* – note that they considered this the 4th killing in Whitechapel]

Annie was 47-years old, 5 feet tall with dark brown hair and a large thick nose. She was wearing a black figured jacket, brown bodice, black skirt, and lace boots. Her health was poor. She had been given medication for what was thought to be lung disease from which it is estimated she would have a life expectancy of just a few months. She was married to John Chapman, a coachman, by whom she had had 3 children. He had died in 1886 and since then she had been living at a common lodging house at No. 30 Dorset Street with the sieve-maker for whom she worked.

As with Polly Nichols (see page 18), Annie's last movements are well documented. At 2 a.m. she had spoken with Timothy Donovan, the deputy of a lodging house at No. 35 Dorset Street, and just like Polly she was drunk, and being without money to pay for a bed for the night was asked to leave. However, she was equally confident that she would return later. A John Richardson of No. 2 John Street was sitting on the steps leading to the backyard where Annie's body was found at around 4.45 a.m. and saw nothing.

[Contemporary photographs of the murder site at No. 29 Hanbury Street along with the mortuary photograph of Annie Chapman]

A little later Albert Cadosch who lived next door at No. 27 Hanbury Street went into his backyard (which was separated from No. 29 by a fence that was 5 feet high) and heard voices, but could not make any part of the conversation out except the word 'No'. He went out again at 5.28 a.m. as he heard a noise as if something was falling against the fence, and 2 minutes later a Mrs. Elizabeth Long saw a man and a woman (almost certainly Annie) in Hanbury Street close to The Alma public house. She was able to describe the man as being foreign, with dark hair and wearing a deerstalker hat and a dark overcoat – overall he was of 'shabby-genteel' appearance. Finally, at 6 a.m. John Davis, a resident at No. 29, was to discover Annie's body close to the back steps and partition fence.

[Today the location of where No. 29 Hanbury Street once stood is occupied by shops built into the edifice of the old Truman Brewery (bottom), while a reminder of the former brewery can be found in Brick Lane (top)]

Her injuries were vividly described by the *East London Observer* – 'a woman lay there with her clothes so disarranged as to expose her knees drawn up as if in agony, together with the lower portion of the abdomen, which had been mutilated in a frightful manner, the intestines, with the viscera and the heart, having been literally torn out of the mangled body and laid by her side. The head of the woman was turned back, revealing an enormous gash, so broad and so deep as almost to have severed the connection with the body. The face – that of a woman of about 40 – was deadly white, and the hair, which was wavy brown, was slightly disarranged. Portions of the flesh on the lower part of the body hung in shreds, the dress was bespattered with blood – as, indeed, was a portion of the fencing, as if it had received a spurt from a severed artery – beside the woman two pools of blood had formed, and upon her shoulders were slashes of blood and some of the viscera. Her head was lying towards the house, and her feet towards the end of the yard'. What was not mentioned was that part of the belly wall, the womb, the upper part of the vagina and the greater part of the bladder were all missing. She had also been partially strangulated – no doubt to make her unconscious while her dissection was performed. In addition, her wedding and keeper (designed to be close fitting and worn on a finger to stop another more valuable ring from slipping off) rings were missing, having been pulled from her fingers.

The conclusions were that both Nichols and Chapman were killed by the same person who possessed some anatomical knowledge, and who latterly wanted to keep some body parts as a sort of trophy. It was also thought that the murder weapon was something like a small, narrow amputating knife, or possibly an implement such as would be used by a slaughterman, of about 6-8 inches in length.

Having been removed by handcart to the mortuary in Montagu Street, Marylebone, Annie was subsequently buried on the 14th September in a communal grave at Manor Park Cemetery, Forest Gate – the same resting ground as Polly Nichols (see page19). The inquest into her death, which took place at the Working Lad's Institute in Whitechapel, commenced on the 10th September and was to last 5 days with the final day adjourned until the 26th September after her funeral. The inevitable verdict was that of wilful murder by person or persons unknown.

On the day of the murder the police acted swiftly: Several officers were placed on plain-clothes duty, interviews were conducted with all the inhabitants of No. 29 Hanbury Street as well as the adjoining houses, common lodging houses in the area were visited to see if anybody had arrived there with blood about their person, pawnbrokers and jewellers visited to see if Annie's missing rings could be traced, public houses visited to get more information about Annie's last movements and any of her clients that night, information circulated about possible suspects etc.

From the 15th September the police investigation was to be under the sole control of Chief Inspector Donald Swanson by order of Sir Charles Warren, the Metropolitan Police Commissioner.

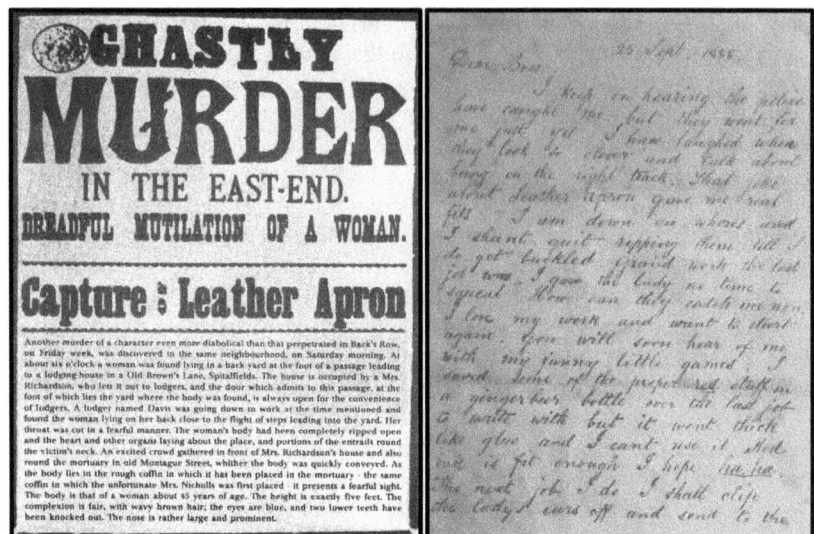

[A 'Leather Apron' poster (left) and the first 'Dear Boss' letter (right)]

As well as normal police enquiries there was also a 'red herring' in the form of a leather apron found in the backyard at No. 29 Hanbury Street with which to contend. It actually belonged to John Richardson, but at the time it fuelled speculation in the press, first mentioned in connection with the murder of Nichols, that the murderer was someone who used a leather apron for work, and most likely of Jewish origin. The hunt for 'Leather Apron' was afoot. One unfortunate individual named John Piser (in some documents Pizer), a 38-year-old Polish Jew who made boots from leather (and was known locally as 'Leather Apron') was arrested on the 10th September. In fact, on the same day as Piser was arrested the police had 7 other suspects in detention. The fact that Piser had 'a cruel and sardonic look', used knives in his work, and used to be taunted by children was enough to make him an immediate suspect despite his having alibis for the nights in question. The accusation was so libellous that he was later able to get compensation from the newspaper that had named him as the prime suspect in the Whitechapel murders.

Suspects were plentiful and included William Piggott (a ship's cook), Friedrich Schumacher, Edward McKenna (an itinerant pedlar), Jacob Isenschmidt (a mentally ill man who had been a pork butcher), Oswald Puckeridge (another mentally ill man who had surgical training, and who had recently been released from an asylum), and an unknown American physician who in 1887 (and probably later in 1888) had offered £20 per fresh body organ i.e. not one that had been preserved in alcohol.

Many suspects were arrested and released because the police still had no firm evidence as to who the murderer was, though they were soon to have his name, for on the 27th September the Central News Agency was to receive the first 'Dear Boss' letter signed 'Jack the Ripper' (which was not published until after the 'double event' of the 30th September 1888 – see page 29). In it he wrote of 'that joke about Leather Apron gave me the fits'. The name of Jack the Ripper was to stick thereafter. In fact, current thinking is that the 'Dear Boss' letter was a fake sent by a reporter, being written by an educated person trying to give the impression of being an illiterate one.

The police advised that prostitutes should walk in pairs, and carry whistles. Further they placed an extra 27 plain-clothes officers on the beat and drafted in other officers as from 1st October. There were also suggestions that Scotland Yard should disguise men as women prostitutes, have boxers dressed as women and with steel collars, and that the eyes of the victims should be photographed (in the belief that the retina captured and retained the last image the victims saw).

The police were doing all that they could but were being hampered, for as Sir Charles Warren reported in a letter to the Home Office, 'moreover the reporters for the press are following our detectives about everywhere in search of news and cross examine all parties interviewed so that they impede police action greatly'. He also stated his frustration that, 'no progress has as yet been made in obtaining any definite clue to the Whitechapel murders. A great number of clues have been examined and exhausted without finding any thing suspicious. A large staff of men are employed and every point is being examined which seems to offer any prospect of a discovery'.

[Just two of the cartoons that hinted at police incompetence]

27

The press was becoming increasingly unkind to the police with allegations of incompetence at every level. The Minister of Parliament for Whitechapel, Samuel Montagu, wanted to offer a £100 reward for information, but was refused permission by the Home Secretary, and in desperation some locals set up the Whitechapel Vigilance Committee.

The police with all their extra officers might well have thought that they were prepared for any further atrocity ... but they were to be proved spectacularly wrong on the 30th September 1888 – the day of the 'double event'.

HANBURY STREET

[Hanbury Street, in the late 19th century, would have looked similar to Dorset Street (above) with its many lodging and public houses]

Formerly Browne's Lane (being originally named after the developer of the area in the 17th century), Hanbury Street runs off Commercial Street, across Brick Lane, to the junction with Old Montague Street and Vallance Road in Spitalfields. It was from a small house here in 1884 that Florence Soper, the daughter-in-law of William Booth (founder of The Salvation Army), ran the newly inaugurated Women's Social Work. It was both a safe haven for prostitutes as well as a place where it was hoped they would be able to turn away from that trade. The south side of the street (between Commercial Street and Brick Lane) with its flats above and shops below has changed little since Victorian times, though the north side was demolished to make way for the extension of the Truman Black Eagle Brewery. The brewery closed in 1989 and today the site is an arts and event centre. The entertainer Bud Flanagan was born at No. 12 in 1896.

28

ELIZABETH STRIDE (SUNDAY 30TH SEPTEMBER 1888)

[Various drawings from *The Illustrated Police News*]

The 3rd canonical victim of Jack the Ripper was Elizabeth Stride (maiden name Elizabeth Gustafsdotter), also known as 'Long Liz' on account of her height/long legs. She was destined to meet her end at 1.00 a.m. in Dutfield's Yard, No. 40 Berner Street (now Henriques Street) which was adjacent to the International Working Men's Educational Club (IWMEC). The IWMEC is long gone having been replaced by the Harry Gosling Primary School – the murder spot is somewhere towards the middle of the playground.

Elizabeth was Swedish by birth but spoke almost perfect English and Yiddish, was 44-years old, had been married to a carpenter named John Stride, and apart from cleaning and other domestic work supplemented her income through prostitution. Elizabeth had run a coffee shop in Upper North Street, and later in Poplar High Street while living with her husband in East India Dock Road. However, after her marriage broke down in 1877, she had been an inmate at the Poplar workhouse before moving to a common lodging house at No. 32 Flower and Dean Street.

Unfortunately, Elizabeth was a bit of a fantasist, so much of what is reported about her may be false e.g. she claimed to have had 9 children though she is only known to have had one stillborn child in 1865. She also stated, maybe out of pride, that her husband and children had drowned in the *Princess Alice* disaster of 1878, when, in fact, John Stride was to die of heart disease in Bromley some 6 years later. More recently she had been living in Devonshire Street with Michael Kidney, a waterside labourer, but seems to have parted company with him since on the 27th September 1888 she was back at the common lodging house in Flower and Dean Street.

[Berner Street, now Henriques Street, showing the entrance to Dutfield's Yard – where the wheel is affixed to the wall of the building (top and bottom left), and the same site in 2020 – the body was found in what is now the middle of the school playground (bottom right)]

On the night of her death Elizabeth was seen drinking in the Queen's Head public house at around 6.30 p.m. with Elizabeth Tanner, the deputy at the lodging house.

She was wearing an old black skirt, black jacket trimmed with fur and with a posy of a red rose in a spray with either a fern or asparagus leaves pinned to it, a checked neckerchief, and a black crêpe bonnet.

[Contemporary illustration of the common lodging house in Flower and Dean Street where Elizabeth Stride resided (top left), which today would have stood just past the large iron gates on the left-hand side of what is now Lolesworth Street (bottom), and a Victorian photograph of another common lodging house in Flower and Dean Street (top right)]

There were 3 other possible sightings of her with clients in Berner Street around 11.00 p.m., 11.45 p.m., and 12.45 a.m. respectively. The last witness was Israel Schwartz who said that he had seen a man speaking to a woman in the gateway of the IWMEC and that the man had thrown the woman down onto the pavement. There was also another man across the street lighting a pipe, and when the attacker saw this person he shouted out 'Lipski' (see page 92). Not wishing to get involved he had run away from the scene. Finally, 10 minutes earlier Police Constable William Smith had seen Elizabeth with a man opposite the IWMEC.

By midnight many of the members had left the IWMEC, with only around 20-30 remaining to talk and sing. There was no light in the yard. Elizabeth's body was found by the IWMEC's steward, Louis Diemschutz, who lived on the premises, but had been out that evening. He returned at 1.00 a.m., and as he drove his pony and cart into the yard, he came across a 'bundle on the ground' by the gateway which upon inspection was found to be Elizabeth's body. The alarm was raised and soon the police were at the scene. All the IWMEC members still present were searched and had their statements taken. Others who had been there earlier in the evening were also interviewed, but none had seen a body as late as 12.50 a.m. on the morning in question.

[Mortuary photograph of Elizabeth Stride]

Excerpts from the police surgeon's report stated that 'the body was lying on the near side, with the face turned toward the wall, the head up the yard and the feet toward the street. The left arm was extended and there was a packet of cachous (lozenges to mask bad breath) in the left hand ... The right arm was over the belly; the back of the hand and wrist had on it clotted blood. The legs were drawn up with the feet close to the wall. The body and face were warm and the hand cold. The legs were quite warm ... The throat was deeply gashed, and there was an abrasion of the skin about one and a quarter inches in diameter, apparently stained with blood, under her right brow. ... There was a clear-cut incision on the neck.

It was six inches in length and commenced two and a half inches in a straight line below the angle of the jaw, three quarters of an inch over an undivided muscle, and then, becoming deeper, dividing the sheath. The cut was very clean and deviated a little downwards ...'.

It was concluded that she had been pulled backwards and onto the ground by her neckerchief, the knot of which was tight, before having her throat cut with a single slash as she was pinned to the ground. However, the injuries lacked the gruesomeness of those of Annie Chapman (see page 21) so it is thought that Jack the Ripper was disturbed, and did not have enough time to complete his work. Some claim that this was not a Jack the Ripper murder for (a) there was a lack of injuries, (b) it was the only murder committed south of the Whitechapel Road, and (c) the police surgeon's report established that the wounds were from a knife with a shorter blade than had been used previously.

Elizabeth was buried the following Saturday at the East London Cemetery, Plaistow.

Following the murder, the police did their best against hostility from newspapers and other quarters. In today's terms they were hampered by 'the management of ignorance', the investigation was producing too many avenues of enquiry with witness statements often contradicting each other.

Chief Inspector Swanson reported that 80,000 leaflets appealing for public information relating to Elizabeth's death had been distributed, and that in just one strand of the investigation, around 2,000 lodgers had been interviewed. The police desperately needed to prioritise their lines of enquiry, rather than trying to follow up on every lead. Matters were not made any easier when there was a second murder that morning ...

THE *PRINCESS ALICE* DISASTER

On the 3rd September 1878 the worst inland waterway disaster in British history took place as the *Princess Alice* paddle steamer made her way back to London following a day trip to Sheerness. As the paddle steamer came round the corner from Tripcock Point and entered Gallions Reach at approximately 7.30 p.m. she was confronted by the much larger *Bywell Castle*, a collier 5 times the weight of the *Princess Alice*, coming in the other direction. Both ships tried to take avoiding action but it was too late for the 640 plus lives that were lost that day. A diver later reported that bodies appeared to be filling the vessel's cabins and could be seen in a standing position, crammed around the exit points as they had tried in vain to escape.

The subsequent enquiry found that both vessels were too slow to act, and to make matters worse the *Princess Alice* was overloaded with 900 passengers on a vessel that should have held no more than 500 persons. A recommendation was made that there should be 'proper and stringent rules and regulations ... laid down for all stream navigation on the River Thames', for up until then there was only the poorly publicised Thames Conservancy Board regulations of 1872 that stated that such vessels should 'port her helm'.

CATHERINE EDDOWES (SUNDAY 30TH SEPTEMBER 1888)

[Drawings from *The Illustrated Police News* and *The Penny Illustrated Paper* covering the murder of Catherine Eddowes]

Like Elizabeth Stride (see page 29), Catherine Eddowes was also living at a common lodging house at Flower and Dean Street (No. 55). As well as Eddowes, she used the surname Kelly (after her current partner John Kelly) and Thomas Conway (after her ex-partner with whom she had had 3 children). She was 46-years old and one of 11 children herself, and although John Kelly claimed that Catherine was not a prostitute all the evidence points to her being one (occasional or otherwise), though both of them had just returned from paid work hop-picking in Kent the previous Thursday. She was originally from Birmingham and had a reputation for being both cheerful and singing all the time, as well as having a fierce temper. Catherine was 5 feet tall, with dark auburn hair and hazel eyes.

On the 29th September Catherine told John that she was going over to see her daughter Annie Phillips who lived in Bermondsey (south of the river) in an attempt to get some money since that she had earned hop-picking had already been spent. John was to pawn his boots so that he could afford a place in a common lodging house that night. It is not known whether Catherine made that journey, or was successful in obtaining any money, but her next sighting was at 8.30 p.m. that night when she was found drunk in Aldgate High Street by Police Constable Louis Robinson. Not being able to ascertain where she lived, he, along with another officer, took Catherine to Bishopsgate police station where she was placed in a cell until she was thought sober enough to leave. That was at 1.00 a.m. when the police station inspector ordered her to be released. Some references state that she was let go because the police officers had grown tired of her endless singing – this is pure speculation as there is no evidence to suggest that she was in any a fit state to sing.

[The original Bishopsgate police station designed by Sir Horace Jones (who was also responsible for Tower Bridge, Smithfield and Leadenhall Markets) dating from 1866 (left), and the current building constructed on the same site and opened in 1939 just prior to World War II during which it received a direct hit from a German bombing raid, but due to it being structurally reinforced remained virtually undamaged (right)]

At that time, she gave her name as Mary Ann Kelly with an address in Fashion Street. It was noted that she was wearing a black straw bonnet trimmed with green and black velvet, a black cloth jacket with imitation fur, a chintz skirt with a pattern of daisies and golden lilies, a grey stuff petticoat, an old green alpaca skirt and another even older blue skirt underneath, a neckerchief of red gauze, and an apron. When she left the police station it was raining. She did not go in the direction of Flower and Dean Street (probably because she had no money for her lodging) but in the opposite direction toward the City. Three men saw her at 1.35 a.m. talking with another man at the entrance to Church Passage close to Mitre Square. It was the unfortunate Police Constable Edward Watkins who was to find her body some 10 minutes later in the southwest corner of the square.

[A contemporary photograph of the southwest corner of Mitre Square where the body of Catherine Eddowes was found (top) and looking along the south side of the square in 2020 (bottom)]

There was a tea warehouse in the square but the night watchman, an ex-police officer himself, said he had seen and heard nothing, and neither had the night watchman at No. 5, or the off-duty police officer who resided at No. 3. Just after 2.00 a.m. Dr. Frederick Brown was at the scene and in his subsequent report he stated that, 'the body was on its back, the head turned to her left shoulder. The arms by the side of the body as if they had fallen there ... The clothes drawn up above the abdomen. The thighs were naked ... The throat cut across ... below the throat was a neckerchief ... The intestines were drawn out to a large extent and placed over the right shoulder – they were smeared over with some feculent matter. A piece of about two feet was quite detached from the body and placed between the body and the left arm, apparently by design. The lobe and auricle of the right ear were cut obliquely through. There was a quantity of clotted blood on the pavement on the left side of the neck round the shoulder and upper part of the arm, and fluid blood-coloured serum which had flowed under the neck to the right shoulder, the pavement sloping in that direction ... The peritoneal lining was cut through on the left side and the left kidney carefully taken out and removed ... I believe the perpetrator of the act must have had considerable knowledge of the position of the organs in the abdominal cavity and the way of removing them ... It required a great deal of knowledge to have removed the kidney and to know where it was placed. Such a knowledge might be possessed by one in the habit of cutting up animals. I think the perpetrator of this act had sufficient time ... It would take at least five minutes. ... I believe it was the act of one person.' As well as the missing kidney part of her apron was also absent.

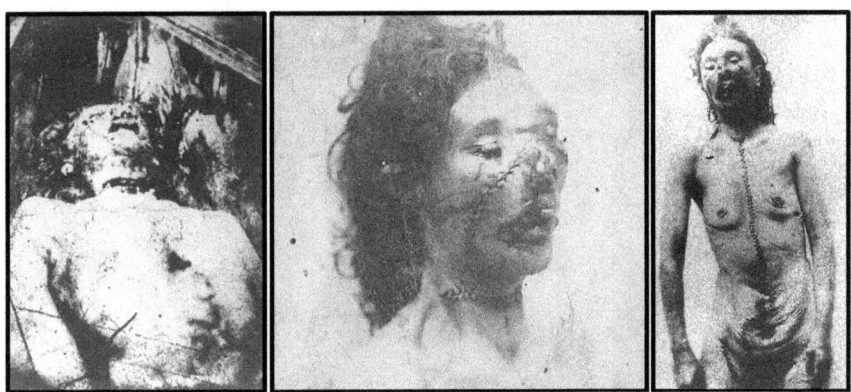

[Mortuary photographs of Catherine Eddowes]

Later Dr. Thomas Bond, the police physician (who was also involved with the Mary Kelly, Catherine Mylett, and Alice McKenzie investigations – see pages 48, 74, and 77 respectively), was to disagree with the latter statements as to the murderer's skill level. He stated that, 'in each case the mutilation was inflicted by a person who had no scientific nor anatomical knowledge. In my opinion he does not even possess the technical knowledge of a butcher or horse slaughterer or any person accustomed to cut up dead animals'. Dr. William Saunders, the Public Analyst for the City of London, agreed in that he believed that Jack the Ripper was not looking to take any particular organ, and just happened upon the left kidney (and part of the womb) which were cut out with no significant anatomical skill.

The knife used was estimated to be one with a blade of 6 inches in length and therefore similar to that used in the Elizabeth Stride killing (see page 32). The murder was the first one not to take place in the East End, but within the bounds (just) of the City of London, and therefore under the jurisdiction of the City of London police (who had also placed extra patrols about the area). Hence the investigation was made in conjunction with the Metropolitan Police enquiries, and was to result in the production of some excellent crime scene drawings and plans of the vicinity. The general area was immediately searched with the result that at around 3.00 a.m. Police Constable Alfred Long found the missing fragment from Catherine's apron, stained with blood and faecal matter, lying in the passage of the doorway leading to Nos. 108 and 119 Model Dwellings, Goulston Street, Whitechapel. Above it on the wall, and written in chalk, were the words, 'The Juwes are The men that Will not be Blamed for nothing'.

[Goulston Street on a busy Sunday morning]

This is known to 'Ripperologists' as the Goulston Street graffito, and is perceived as a vital clue, and one which upon the orders of Sir Charles Warren (at the suggestion of Police Superintendent Thomas Arnold) was washed away before being photographed. The reason given was that with dawn approaching the police did not want to incite a riot in this mainly Jewish district, especially at a time when tensions were at a peak.

[The Model Dwellings in Goulston Street with shops below (left) and what used to be the entrance where the graffito was written in chalk, and also where the missing fragment of apron was found (right)]

By the 2nd October the police had pieced together from various interviews a general description of Jack the Ripper as being 'of shabby appearance, about 30 years of age and 5 feet 9 inches in height, of fair complexion, having a small fair moustache and a cap with a peak'.

The newspapers were quick to criticise the police efforts, and the general public flooded the police with letters suggesting lines of enquiry that might be taken e.g. Jack the Ripper escapes via the sewers, he disguises himself as a policeman, that a gang might be responsible, the murderer is a watchman etc. Jack the Ripper also wrote his famous 'Saucy Jack' postcard sent on the 1st October 1888. Like the 'Dear Boss' letter a few days earlier (see page 26) it was viewed as being a fraud, but it did not stop the newspapers publishing both of them (and in so doing increasing their circulation) – the only real effect publication had was that it led to other hoax letters being sent which were to take up valuable police time and resources.

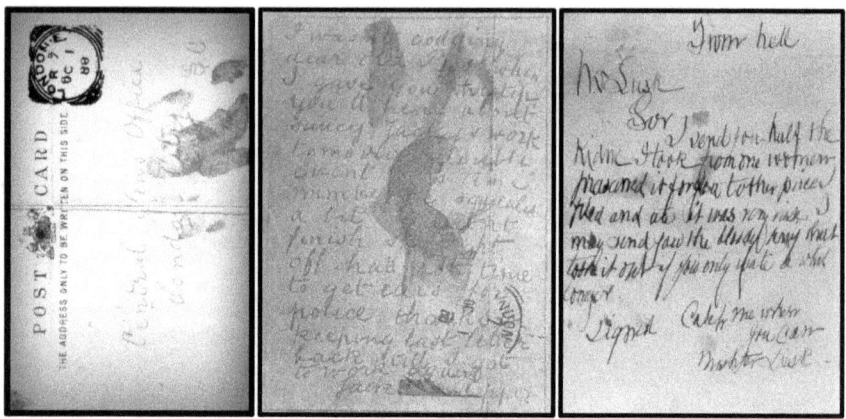

[The 'Saucy Jack' postcard (left and centre), and 'From Hell' letter (right)]

On the 16th October George Lusk, the chairman of the Whitechapel Vigilance Committee, received the 'From Hell' letter along with a portion of a human kidney – the other half, the letter claimed, had been eaten by Jack the Ripper. At first it was thought that the letter was genuine for the kidney did match the one missing from Catherine's body i.e. had the correct length of renal artery where it had been severed, and had Bright's disease. However, later evidence shows that the kidney had been trimmed, the renal artery was entirely absent, and it had been placed in preservative – the conclusion was that the kidney had been obtained from a hospital morgue and been sent, most likely, by a medical student as a prank.

Catherine was buried on the 8th October in the City of London Cemetery in Manor Park.

In the weeks that followed the police continued their investigations much as before, only with even more men at their disposal. More leaflets were printed, a reward of £500 was now offered from the Corporation of the City of London, the two police forces had daily meetings, various properties were searched, arrests made, suspects interviewed, patrols stepped up to a frequency of every 15 minutes, and even two bloodhounds (Barnaby and Burgho) were assessed over 2 days in Regent's Park and Hyde Park for their ability to follow a scent should another murder occur. The newspapers were now even more critical of the police, running headlines such as *The Headless Criminal Investigation Department* and

Why Detectives Don't Detect. Mitre Square, in particular, was becoming a tourist attraction with sightseers wanting to view where the murder took place. Some 4,000 women signed a petition to Queen Victoria, and the police received 1,500 letters of help along with some confessions. Even Sir Arthur Conan Doyle, the creator of Sherlock Holmes, was asked for his opinion/expertise.

[3 more drawings from *The Illustrated Police News* highlighting the desperation of the police enquiry. Spiritualist theories were entertained (left), bloodhounds were assessed for their tracking abilities – and although 3 dogs are shown only 2, Barnaby and Burgho, were actually tried out (middle), and Sir Charles Warren viewed the Goulston Street graffito prior to his order to have it removed (right)]

In a letter written on the 23rd October 1888 to the Home Secretary, Robert Anderson (who was by then the head of the CID as well as being the Assistant Commissioner) expresses his frustration thus: 'I wish to guard against its being supposed that the inquiry is now concluded ... that a crime of this kind should have been committed without any clue being supplied by the criminal, is unusual, but that 5 (he was counting Martha Tabram – see page 65 – as a Jack the Ripper victim) successive murders should have been committed without our having the slightest clue of any kind is extraordinary, if not unique, in the annals of crime. The result has been to necessitate our giving attention to innumerable suggestions, such as would in any ordinary case be dismissed unnoticed ... moreover, the activity of the Police has been to a considerable extent wasted through the exigencies of sensational journalism, and the action of unprincipled persons, who, from various motives, have endeavoured to mislead us. But on the other hand the public generally and especially the inhabitants of the East End have shown a remarkable desire to assist in every way, even at some sacrifice to themselves ... the vigilance of the officers engaged on the inquiry continues unabated'.

October came and went without incident, but then just as some thought that the Jack the Ripper attacks were over ...

HOPPING

[A rush of hop-pickers at Holborn Viaduct station]

The flowers of the hop plant have been used in the brewing of beer in England since they were first introduced in the 16th century by Dutch farmers. The plants are trained to grow up strings between poles, and because of this harvesting is a very labour-intensive affair. When the hop-picking season was about to commence London railway stations would see a surge of men, women, and children, with baskets and tins, and kettles and sacks, making their way on special trains, which since the 1870s, had been timetabled to transport whole families to Kent. Invariably the passengers came from the slums of the East End, though some would be artisans or out of work factory girls in search of a change for a few weeks. In exchange for hard work picking the hops they would be given food, shelter, a little money, and hopefully some sunshine too. For most it was considered something of a holiday, a break from the semi-starvation of a slum, spent away from the narrow courts and filthy alleys of the East End.

MODEL DWELLINGS

In the late Victorian period the millions of London inhabitants were housed in approximately 700,000 houses. For the East End poor it might be a tenement where one room would take the place of all the rooms to be found in the houses of the more affluent West End residents. This, however, changed in the 1860s when large, austere, barrack-like structures some 5 or 6 storeys in height, often with tiers of iron balconies running along the face of the buildings, began to appear. This was the beginning of the class of building known as Model Dwellings which were intended for 'the artisan and labouring poor of London'.

[An East End single-roomed tenement (left) and Model Dwelling (right)]

The first was the result of a trust set up by the American philanthropist George Peabody, who in March 1862 gave an initial £150,000 to endow a fund 'to ameliorate the condition of the poor and needy of this great metropolis and to promote their comfort and happiness'. The Peabody Donation Fund was in part used to provide 'cheap, cleanly, well-drained and healthful dwellings for the poor'. The first such development, which was opened in 1864, was in Commercial Street, Spitalfields. Other Peabody Trust developments soon followed so that by 1890 some 5,000 dwellings had been built – today the trust administers some 20,000 rented homes on a number of estates in inner London. Peabody was not alone for soon there were also other similar organisations set up, e.g. Octavia Hill, The East End Dwelling Company, the Improved Industrial Dwelling Company, and The Guinness Trust. The London County Council even got involved. Each organisation worked on a requirement to make a small annual profit on rents, usually of the order of 5%, which would then be used to build more such properties.

The Goulston Street Model Dwellings, known formerly as Wentworth Dwellings, dating from 1887 were 5 storeys tall and contained 222 residences in total. At the time of Jack the Ripper the flats were predominantly inhabited by Jews (95% plus) giving credence to the decision by Sir Charles Warren to have the antisemitic graffito removed. By the 1970s the residents were mainly Bengali immigrants living in appalling conditions. In fact, the local council placed a compulsory purchase order on the building with a view to demolition. The dwellings were cleared of occupants and the entrances bricked up in 1982. However, in 1990 it was decided that a better alternative was to refurbish the building which today is known as Merchant House.

MARY KELLY (FRIDAY 9TH NOVEMBER 1888)

[Coverage of the Mary Kelly murder as printed in *The Illustrated Police News* who considered her the 7th victim of Jack the Ripper]

The death of Mary Kelly was different from the previous 4 murders and some 'Ripperologists' believe that it should not be attributed to Jack the Ripper. For a start Mary was far younger than the other victims at just 25-years old. It was also the only murder to take place indoors (at No. 13 Miller's Court at the back of No. 26 Dorset Street, Spitalfields where she lived), and it took place over 5 weeks after the previous murder with the mutilations being far in excess of anything seen thus far.

Mary, who also went by the names Marie Jeanette, 'Fair' Emma, 'Ginger', 'Dark' Mary and 'Black' Mary, was born in Ireland (probably Limerick) but like Elizabeth Stride (see page 29) was prone to flights of fantasy. Hence, she may/may not have lived in Wales where she married a coal miner named Davis or Davies, been disowned by her parents, come from a moderately wealthy family, had 7 brothers and a sister, had a family member on the London theatrical stage, been well educated, and was/was not a good artist.

[Mary Kelly]

She was reported as being a blonde, or a redhead – which rather contradicts her being known as 'Black' Mary or 'Ginger' – 5 feet 7 inches in height, slim, attractive and with a fresh complexion. The 'Dark' Mary title comes from the fact that while resident in the East End she took to drinking heavily after which she would start to sing Irish songs and become generally abusive and unpleasant.

In approximately 1884 she moved to London and worked in Chelsea, and Fitzrovia in the West End, where she became a high-class prostitute working out of a brothel.

Mary was very popular and one client even took her to France. Afterwards she adopted the French name Marie Jeanette. However, there must have been a downturn in her life, for a year later she was to be found in the East End, lodging in the Ratcliffe Highway, and later in Stepney, before ending up at a lodging house in Thrawl Street, Spitalfields. It was here she met, and became partner to, a fish porter at Billingsgate Market called Joseph Barnett. They lived together in George Street, then Little Paternoster Row, followed by a period in Brick Lane (see page 64) before finally settling in Dorset Street in early 1888. At the time of her murder Mary and Joseph were not together, having argued a week before about Mary letting other prostitutes use their dwelling – there was also friction between them because Joseph had recently lost his job which forced Mary back onto the streets.

On the evening of the 8th September 1888 it was raining hard. Joseph visited Mary at Miller's Court at around 7.00 p.m. and found her with Maria Harvey. They were joined by another prostitute, Lizzie Albrook, before Joseph and Maria left together. At that time Mary was sober, but later in the evening she was seen in the company of Elizabeth Foster at the Ten Bells public house on the corner of Commercial Street and Fournier Street, Spitalfields, and later still with 2 other people at the Horn of Plenty public house in Dorset Street. Mary Cox, another prostitute and resident at No. 5 Miller's Court, saw her return drunk to Miller's Court at 11.45 p.m. with a man/client.

[The Ten Bells public house]

[The entrance to Miller's Court (top left), and Mary Kelly's abode at No. 13 Miller's Court (top right), and the same redeveloped locations in 2020 showing the Spitalfields Fruit & Wool Exchange building (bottom left), and the atrium (bottom right)]

Kelly could be heard singing in her room as late as 1.00 a.m., but by 1.30 a.m. the singing, according to Elizabeth Prater who lived directly above, had stopped. Elizabeth also said that she (corroborated Sarah Lewis who was sleeping at No. 2 Miller's Court) heard a faint cry of 'Murder' between 3.30 a.m. and 4.00 a.m. but had taken no notice of it at the time since such cries were common in the area. Cox also thought that she heard somebody leaving Mary's room at 5.45 a.m.

There was a separate sighting of Mary at 2.00 a.m. by a man named George Hutchinson who stated that he met Mary at Flower and Dean Street, after which she went off in the direction of Thrawl Street where she was approached by a wealthy-looking man of Jewish appearance. Hutchinson was suspicious of this person who looked so out of place in the area. Consequently, he kept watch on them both until 2.45 a.m. at which point they had been inside No. 13 Miller's Court for some time. Once again, Sarah Lewis was able to partially verify these latter movements as she confirmed seeing a drunk man and women in the courtyard at 2.30 a.m.

[Whatever the weather, The Lord Mayor's Show, a free spectacle within the City of London, always attracts large crowds]

On the morning of the 9th November it was still raining which was a pity for all those involved in the Lord Mayor's Show that day. It was going to be a day to remember for Thomas Bowyer, an assistant to Mary Kelly's landlord John McCarthy, when he was sent around to No. 13 Miller's Court to collect the rent arrears (6 weeks). It was just after 10.45 a.m. when he knocked on the door to no reply. Not being deterred, he then pushed aside the clothing covering a broken windowpane and saw the mutilated body of Mary on the bed.

The police were called and were soon on the scene, among them were Police Superintendent Thomas Arnold, Police Inspector Edmund Reid (who was also involved in the Emma Smith, Martha Tabram, and Alice McKenzie investigations – see pages 62, 65, and 77 respectively), Police Inspector Frederick Abberline (who had been seconded to Whitechapel from the Central Office at Scotland Yard after the murder of Polly Nichols – see page 15), and Assistant Commissioner Robert Anderson. The bloodhounds Barnaby and Burgho (see page 40) were called for but by now the scent had gone cold. It was noted that women's clothes had been burnt in the fireplace, presumably to give more light for Jack the Ripper to carry out his mutilations – the only other form of light in the room at night-time being a single candle. News travelled fast and it is estimated 1,000 people soon gathered in Dorset Street, with many of them voicing their disapproval of the police investigation to date.

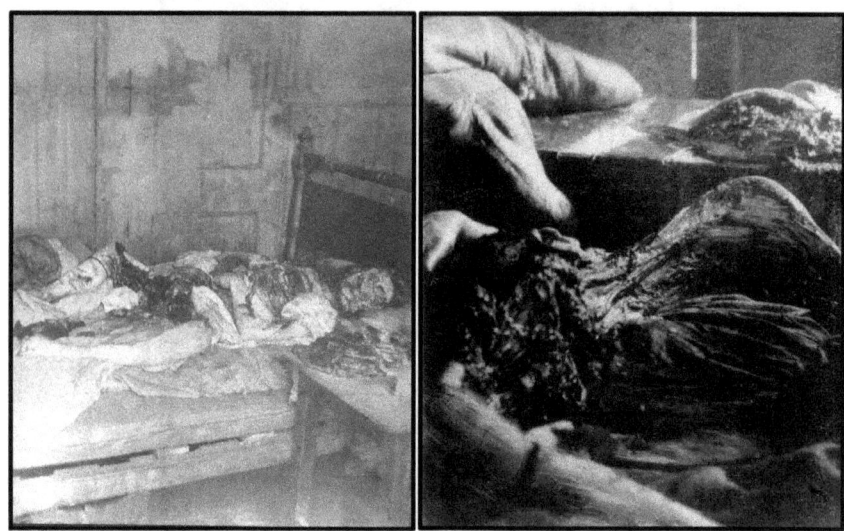

[The 2 crime scene photographs taken of Mary Kelly]

Two crime scene photographs were taken and the body removed via a horse-drawn wagon to the mortuary in Shoreditch. This time the body was examined jointly by Dr. Thomas Bond (who was also involved with the Catherine Eddowes, Catherine Mylett, and Alice McKenzie investigations – see pages 37, 74, and 77 respectively) and Dr. Bagster Phillips (who would be involved with the Alice McKenzie, and Frances Coles murders – see pages 77, and 84 respectively). The mutilations were so severe that Phillips suggested that it would have taken Jack the Ripper 2 hours to complete, though he did not believe that the person responsible showed any signs of medical or anatomical training. The implement used was a knife, around 6 inches long and 1 inch wide, a statement which is in accord with the knife used in the previous murders.

The subsequent post-mortem stated that 'The body was lying naked in the middle of the bed ... the legs were wide apart, the left thigh at right angles to the trunk and the right forming an obtuse angle with the pubis. The whole of the surface of the abdomen and thighs was removed and the abdominal cavity emptied of its viscera. The breasts were cut off, the arms mutilated by several jagged wounds and the face hacked beyond recognition of the features. The tissues of the neck were severed all round down to the bone. The viscera were found in various parts viz. the uterus and kidneys with one breast under the head, the other breast by the right foot, the liver between the feet, the intestines by the right side and the spleen by the left side of the body. The flaps removed from the abdomen and thighs were on a table. The bed clothing at the right corner was saturated with blood, and on the floor beneath was a pool of blood covering about two feet square ... The face was gashed in all directions, the nose, cheeks, eyebrows, and ears being partly removed. The lips were blanched and cut by several incisions running obliquely down to the chin. There were also numerous cuts extending irregularly across all the features ... Both breasts were more or less removed by circular incisions, the muscle down to the ribs being attached to the breasts ...'. In fact, unlike the other victims, it was remarked that Mary's body had not been ripped open, but sliced.

[Shoreditch Town Hall where Mary Kelly's inquest was held]

The inquest at Shoreditch Town Hall produced no new evidence, though in his report Dr. Bond did give a profile of the type of person the police were looking for as being a 'quite likely inoffensive looking man probably middle-aged and neatly and respectably dressed. I think he must be in the habit of wearing a cloak or overcoat or he could hardly have escaped notice in the streets if the blood on his hands and clothes were visible'. It was this statement more than any other that has given rise to the image of Jack the Ripper being a gentleman in a top hat with a cloak and cane. Dr. Bond further said that the perpetrator was most likely a solitary, eccentric individual who was subject to periodic attacks of homicidal and erotic mania, who had been in an extreme state of satyriasis as he performed his mutilations.

Mary was buried on the 19th November 1888 at St. Patrick's Roman Catholic Cemetery in Leytonstone. The inscription on her grave reads, 'In loving memory of Marie Jeanette Kelly. None but the lonely hearts can know my sadness. Love lives forever'.

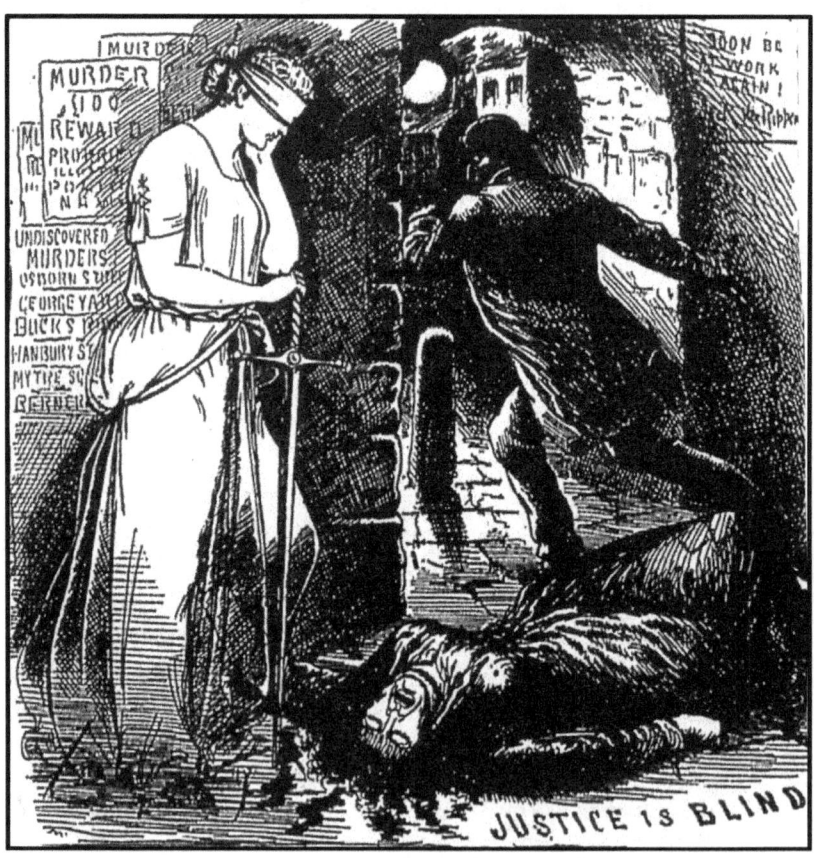

[The press, among many others, blamed the police and their leaders for the failure to bring Jack the Ripper to justice]

The police investigation included extensive questioning of both Joseph Barnett and George Hutchinson (both of whom were regarded as prime suspects) as well as door-to-door searches. A pardon was even offered for anybody who might be considered an accomplice if they came forward with the identity of Jack the Ripper. Sir Charles Warren was also to resign, not over the Whitechapel murders *per se* but over articles he had written attacking government interference in what he considered were police matters. Although he was disliked by the press and the politicians, he was respected by his own men, with virtually every police superintendent on the force visiting him at home to express their support and regret at his departure.

Queen Victoria spoke for many when she was moved to write to the Prime Minister, 'This new most ghastly murder shows the absolute necessity for some very decided action. All these courts must be lit, and our detectives improved. They are not what they should be. You promised, when the first murder took place, to consult with your colleagues about it'.

Many references claim that the police investigation was downsized following Mary's death, but the opposite is true. There were 143 plain-clothes officers involved in the investigation in November and December 1888 (over 100 more officers than in September that year). Taking in all ranks the Whitechapel Division had 585 men on call. It was only after there had been no more victims that the number of police was reduced in the New Year.

As if to prove this point in his end of year report James Monro, who had taken over as Commissioner after the resignation of Sir Charles Warren, stated, 'The agitation which centred in Trafalgar Square, and the murders in Whitechapel, necessitated the concentration in particular localities of large bodies of police, and such an increase of force in one quarter of the Metropolis, it must be remembered, is only procurable by diminishing the number of men ordinarily employed in other divisions'. He went on to complain that because of the extra men in Whitechapel that the consequence was 'diminished numbers of police in other quarters, and so long as the available force is hardly sufficient, as it is just now, for the performance of the ordinary and every day duties of the Police, and an additional drain on its resources leads to a diminished protection against, and consequent increase of, crime'. In his view the police were 'overworked, and under such circumstances crime cannot be met or coped with in a satisfactory and efficient manner'. Finally, with reference to Jack the Ripper specifically he reported his regret that 'in spite of most strenuous efforts on the part of the Police, the criminal has up till now remained undiscovered'.

And that for most 'Ripperologists' was the last of Jack the Ripper, or maybe not ...

SPITALFIELDS

[Spitalfields today with the 18th century Christ Church still dominating the area. The large building to the right is the London Fruit and Wool Exchange which occupies the site where Miller's Court once stood, while to the left is the roof of Spitalfields Market itself]

The fields in question were those to the east of the medieval priory and hospital of St. Mary Spital, where a roman cemetery was discovered in the 16th century. According to Daniel Defoe 'the lanes were deep, dirty and unfrequented, the part now called Spitalfields Market was a field of grass with cows feeding on it. Brick Lane, which is now a long well paved street, was a dirty road, frequented chiefly by carts fetching bricks that way into Whitechapel from brick kilns in those fields'.

In 1537 part of the fields were given over as an artillery ground where members of the Guild of Artillery could practice with their longbows, crossbows and guns. However, this did not last as in 1682 the old artillery ground was purchased by four wealthy property speculators. As early as 1640 buildings had started to appear at the Whitechapel end of the fields, and by 1675 there were around 1,300 small tenements crowded into narrow streets and alleyways. Today the street layout remains virtually unchanged from that of the late 17th century. Artillery Lane is a main thoroughfare leading east from Bishopsgate (the A10) to its junction with Crispin Street and Bell Lane.

A reminder of its former use comes from Gun Street and Fort Street which lead off from Artillery Lane.

[Petticoat Lane, one of 4 important markets in Spitalfields]

In the early 1800s there was an influx of foreigners, especially French weavers, and later Huguenot refugees from France following the revocation of the Edict of Nantes in 1685. Their skill in silk weaving gave the area a reputation for fine-quality cloth and this is remembered in the road names of Fashion Street and Fournier Street (named after the wealthy Huguenot George Fournier).

However, by 1807 when the population was around 15,000 persons, the area had become one of the poorest in London with the properties of the silk merchants, master weavers, dyers, and retailers having given way to common lodging houses. The blocks of new dwellings, including the Peabody buildings in Commercial Street (see page 43), were mainly occupied by Jewish immigrants. As the weaving trade contracted small fruitiers', and clothiers' workshops were set up, as were Truman's Brewery and Spitalfields Market. Since World War II the latest immigrants to settle here have been of Bangladeshi origin, and they have made Brick Lane the curry capital of London. Most recently there has been much redevelopment, with many of the old Georgian housing stock being preserved. This has led to a gentrification of Spitalfields, something which has not necessarily been welcomed by many of the long-standing inhabitants of the area.

CORONER'S COURT

[The purpose-built Poplar Coroner's Court established around 1910]

Once the police had made their report that a death was suspicious it was up to the coroner to take matters further. He would summon a jury, view the body, and investigate how the deceased died by interviewing members of the family and any witnesses. The inquest could be held anywhere, and in Victorian times they were frequently convened in public houses since these premises would have a large table on which a body could be placed, as well as space to accommodate a jury of 12 persons, the coroner, witnesses, and spectators. However, it was still not uncommon for the inquest to be held at the deceased home or even in the open air. Only towards the end of the 19th century did purpose-built mortuaries and courts for coroners start to appear in large towns and cities.

At the time of Jack the Ripper a juror, who would be male since they were picked from the Parliamentary voting lists, was compensated for his time by receiving the sum of 2 shillings a day. Occupants of each street were tasked in turn and attendance could be enforced. If there were multiple cases under review then the juror would have to remain until each of the cases had returned a verdict. A typical inquest would see reporters seated together at a large table. There would be a central witness box, while at the back of the room members of the public would be allowed to watch the proceedings. Also mixed in among the public would be the witnesses, at least those who could control their feelings – others who might be inclined to hysteria would be confined to a waiting room.

[A Coroner's Court at work at the turn of the 20th century (top). As with public hangings Coroner's Courts attracted large crowds waiting to hear the verdict (bottom)]

Once the jury had been sworn in the first order of the day would be to let the jurors view the deceased in the mortuary before any witnesses were called. When all the evidence had been heard the jury would return its verdict, after which the coroner would sign the burial form to release the body to the family of the deceased.

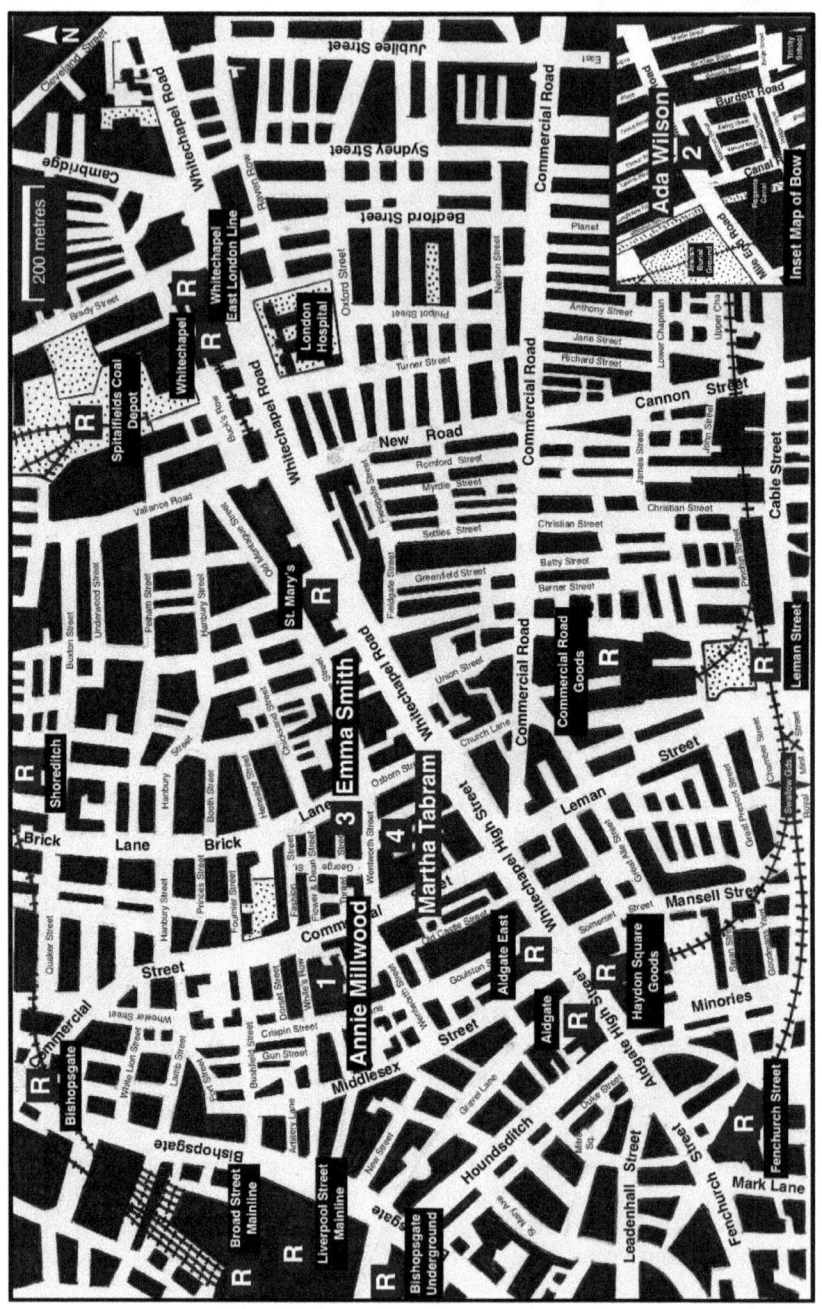

[1888 street map of the 'Genesis' Jack the Ripper Murders (including insert map of Bow which is approx. 1,900 metres from the London Hospital travelling east along Whitechapel Road which later becomes Mile End Road)]

THE GENESIS OF JACK THE RIPPER?

The crime rate in London, and the East End in particular, was such at the time of the Jack the Ripper killings that many other horrific murders of women might, or might not, be part of those crimes that have collectively become known as the Whitechapel Murders and attributed to Jack the Ripper. Here, in chronological order from March to August 1888, are 4 more cases, each deserving a mention if only to illustrate that the East End was a dangerous place to live and work, especially for a woman late at night.

ANNIE MILLWOOD (SATURDAY 25TH FEBRUARY 1888)

[White's Row following bomb damage in 1943 (left), and the location in 2020 of where Spitalfields Chambers once stood (right)]

At the time of her death Annie Millwood was the 38-year old widow of Richard Millwood (a soldier) and lived at Spitalfields Chambers, No. 8 White's Row in Spitalfields (see page 52). There is no evidence to suggest that she was a prostitute. Annie was admitted to the Whitechapel Workhouse Infirmary with stab wounds to her legs and lower part of her abdomen on the 25th February 1888. She claimed to have received the injuries from a man with a clasp knife, though some say that her story was a fabrication and that the wounds were self-inflicted.

She was treated and made a good recovery over the coming weeks. On the 21st March she was sent to the South Grove Workhouse where on the 31st March she was seen to fall to the ground while engaged in 'some occupation' at the rear of the building. She was dead, and according to the subsequent inquest her earlier injuries played no part in her collapse. The cause of death stated by the coroner was a 'sudden effusion into the pericardium from the rupture of the left pulmonary artery through ulceration'. The jury, quite correctly, returned a verdict of death from natural causes.

Some 'Ripperologists' claim the death to be the work of Jack the Ripper who used Millwood to 'learn his trade'. There is also the fact that she was attacked within 'a stone's throw' of where another possible Jack the Ripper victim, Martha Tabram (see page 65), was slain. The death of Annie Millwood is included here to serve as an illustration that such violence against women in the East End was commonplace, though the atrocities in the autumn of 1888 took the murder of women to a whole new level.

WHITE'S ROW

White's Row, which had been known as New Fashion Street, is a narrow road running from east to west from Commercial Street to Crispin Street, which originally formed the boundary of the Wheeler estate to the north and Tenter Ground estate to the south. Structures were built on the land beginning in the 1650s. Many of the properties on the south side were owned by Nathaniel and John Tilly in the late 17th century, and later by the Shepherd family in the late 18th century. A large covered arch, known as Shepherd's Place, was constructed in the early 1800s and became the main entrance to the Tenter Ground estate. By then the area was regarded as a slum with there being several common lodging houses there by the end of the 19th century. World War II saw the western end of the road destroyed by bombing, while in 1963 the northern side of the street was demolished to make way for van and lorry parking, which in 1971 was replaced by a multistorey car park.

ADA WILSON (WEDNESDAY 28TH MARCH 1888)

No. 19 Maidman (in some references Maidmans) Street in Bow was the scene of an attack on the 28th March 1888 just after midnight. Ada Wilson was a seamstress/prostitute (at least her neighbour, Rose Bierman, confirmed that she 'often had visitors to see her') who answered a knock to her front door and was confronted by a man who forced his way in and demanded money before stabbing her twice in the throat. Neighbours nearly caught him as he fled. Ada survived and was able to describe the attacker to the police. He was about 30-years old, 5½ feet tall, had a sunburnt face with a fair moustache, and wore a dark coat, light trousers, and a wide-awake (one with a low crown and a very wide brim) hat.

The Genesis of Jack the Ripper?

[*The Illustrated Police News* drawing of the Ada Wilson attack]

The fact that the assailant was suntanned points to him having been abroad (possibly a sailor), while the type of hat also indicates a foreign person (the style being popular in America and with Quakers). Quite why he picked that particular front door remains a mystery. If he had been a former client, who therefore knew that Ada would be alone and might have money about the house, it could also be supposed that Ada would have recognised him as such. Indeed, there is only her word for it that the man was intent on robbery – it could equally have been an altercation that arose over something sex related. The fact that she said nothing further may have meant that she was trying to conceal something – maybe she did not want to reveal that she was a prostitute, in which case she may have known and feared further reprisals from the attacker. Whatever the truth might be there is little reason for a seamstress to have callers after midnight, unless she was a prostitute and he a client.

There are some 'Ripperologists' who believe that Ada, and Annie Millwood (see page 57) who was stabbed the previous month, were early examples of Jack the Ripper 'learning his trade'. Certainly, the description of the culprit resembles those of Jack the Ripper given to the police during the reign of terror in the autumn of 1888. Having said that this attack is not in the same vicinity, and on the surface appears to have been motivated by money.

Bow

[Bow Bridge spanning the River Lea]

The area of Bow where Ada lived was an important bridgehead on the main road from the East End to Essex over the River Lea. The original Roman crossing had been at Old Ford, but this was inadequate by the 12th century so King Henry I had a new crossing built here. The bridge was shaped like a bow and hence the area's name. Bow became the place where goods, especially grain, brought down the River Lea from Hertfordshire, were unloaded for the London market. With the grain came the opportunity for milling. By the early 14th century Bow was a village with its own church, St. Mary's. It should be pointed out that the 'Bow Bells', which it is said any authentic Cockney is born within the sound of, are not those of St. Mary's in Bow, but those of St. Mary-le-Bow in Cheapside (which were destroyed by bombing in 1941).

Later calico printing and dyeing industries were established along the riverside, and the area also became famous for its blue and white Bow porcelain (though in reality this was produced in nearby Stratford). At the turn of the 19th century Bow's population was around 2,000, but by the middle of the century many more factories (soap, hemp-cloth, rubber, and matches) had been started, and Bow became just another London suburb. In 1875 the Bryant and May match factory employed over 5,600 people, mainly women, and was the scene of the successful 'match-girls' strike for better working conditions in 1888.

The Genesis of Jack the Ripper?

[Mile End Road in the early 20th century with Burdett Road to the left and Guardian Angels Roman Catholic Church to the right (top), and Mile End Park looking across where Maidman Street once ran with the same church in the background (bottom)]

Today the area is a mix of residential and industrial units, both of which have undergone extensive urban regeneration with the impetus of the 2012 Olympic Games at nearby Stratford. Maidman Street ran parallel to the Mile End Road linking Burdett Road and Canal Road close to Mile End Tube station. Maidman Street no longer exists as it is now part of Mile End Park (a 79-acre site which had been planned since the end of World War II, but only became fully possible at the end of the 20th century as part of an early urban redevelopment plan).

EMMA ELIZABETH SMITH (TUESDAY 3ʀᴅ APRIL 1888)

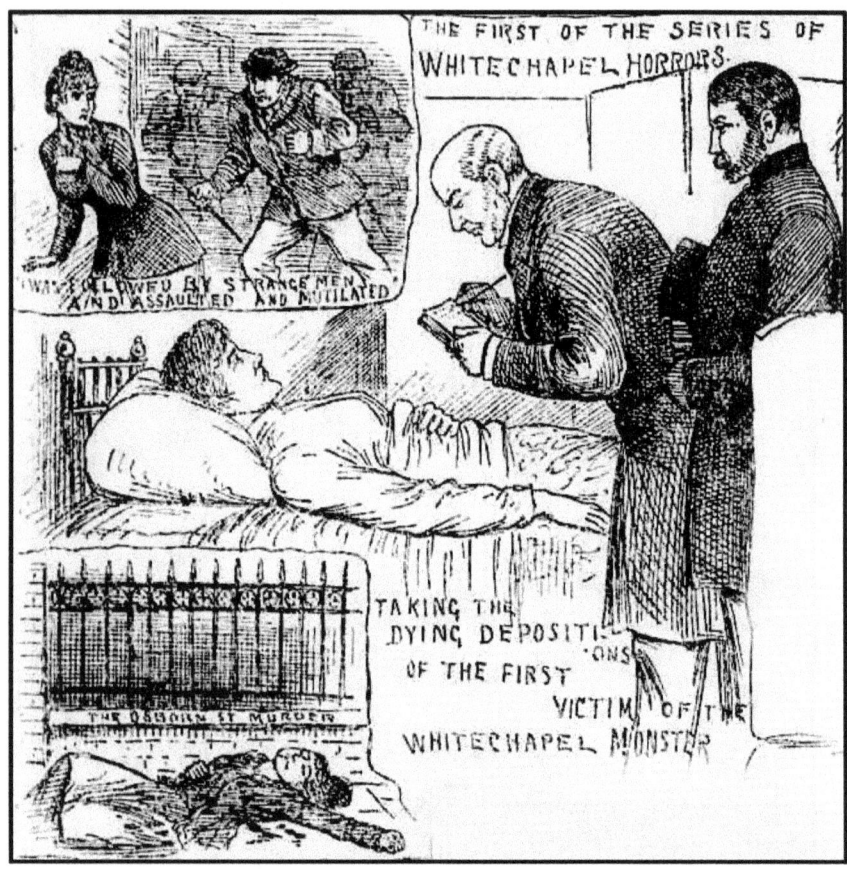

[Drawings from *The Illustrated Police News* of what was described as 'the first of a series of Whitechapel horrors']

Smith was like many women in the area – a prostitute and an alcoholic. She lived in Whitechapel, was 45-years old, and destitute. By all accounts she wandered the streets looking for clients. A police report authored by Detective Inspector Edmund Reid of H Division (who was also to be involved in the Martha Tabram, Mary Kelly, and Alice McKenzie murders – see pages 65, 44, and 76 respectively) on the 16th April 1888 has her as living at a lodging house at No. 18 George Street, Spitalfields (see page 52). She had been resident there for around 18 months. It is thought she was a widow with a son and daughter living somewhere near Finsbury Park. Just after midnight on the 3rd April she had been observed in Limehouse at the junction of Farrance Street and Burdett Road (built in 1862 to connect the riverside hamlets to Victoria Park and named after the philanthropist Angela Burdett-Coutts). She was seen talking to a man (who was not to be a suspect), likely a prospective client, dressed in dark clothes with a white scarf.

[Osborn Street looking toward the junction with Brick Lane, circa 1900 (top), and the same junction in 2020 (bottom)]

Approximately 4 hours later she informed Mary Russell, the deputy-keeper at her lodging house, that she had been assaulted and robbed, and that her 'private parts had been injured'. This attack (often referred to as the Osborn Street Murder) actually took place, according to the police report, opposite No. 10 Brick Lane by Taylor's cocoa factory close to where Brick Lane becomes Osborn Street. This is where just 4 months earlier a friend of hers, Margaret Hames (or Hayes in some references), had been beaten, but not fatally.

The police were not summoned, although she was escorted by Margaret Hames to the London Hospital for examination. It was observed that she had been drinking, but was certainly not drunk. She died at 9 a.m. on the 4th April, with the police not being informed of the death for another 2 days. She had died from her injuries (internal bleeding), which included the 'partition between front and back passage … being broken not cut' likely caused by the thrusting of a blunt object into her vagina. It had penetrated the peritoneum, producing peritonitis. She had used clothing from her shoulders and placed it between her legs to try and arrest the bleeding. There were also wounds to her head and ear.

In this instance it is almost certain that Smith had been the victim of a small gang of youths (she said that one of her attackers was about 19-years old) who had approached her with the intention of robbing her of any money she might have earned that evening. It can only be speculation, but maybe having found she had little money about her person the gang then decided not to rape her, but to 'teach her a lesson' by being sexually sadistic towards her.

BRICK LANE

[Brick Lane in the early 20th century – always a busy street]

The Genesis of Jack the Ripper?

Brick Lane takes its name from the fact that bricks and tiles were manufactured near here from the 16th century. By the middle of the 17th century houses began to appear at the southern end of the lane and a few years later, around 1666, a brewery was built here. The Black Eagle Brewery (better known as Truman's Brewery) was producing 400,000 barrels annually in 1853 (making it the largest in the world). After the partition of Bengal and the Union with Pakistan in 1947 the area became home to many thousands of Bengalis. Today the shops and many restaurants are almost all Bangladeshi. There is also a Saturday market which has its origins in the 18th century when it was a place that farmers could sell their livestock and produce outside the City boundary i.e. without paying City tolls. Today the market is a place for everything from leather goods, jewellery, and kitchenware to books, plants and bric-a-brac.

MARTHA TABRAM (TUESDAY 7TH AUGUST 1888)

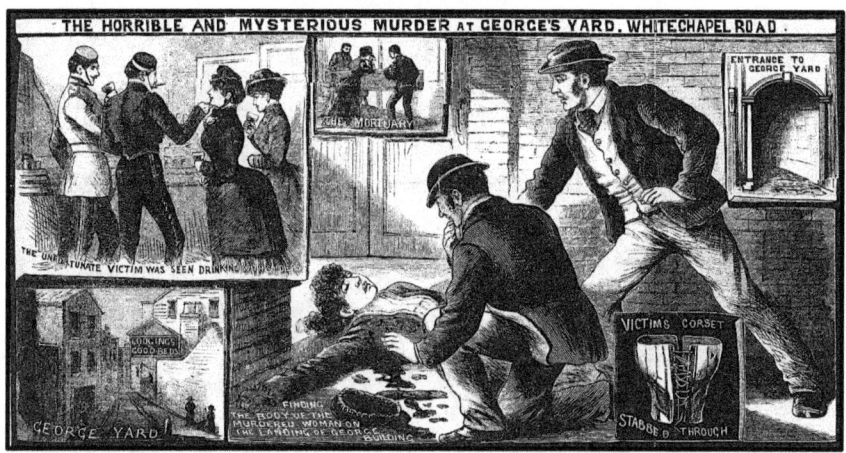

[Drawings from *The Illustrated Police News* concerning Martha Tabram]

In the same month that the Ripper atrocities began the body of Martha Tabram, was found at 4.50 a.m. on Tuesday 7th August 1888 on the first-floor landing of George Yard Buildings (No. 19 George Yard). Martha was 39-years old, an alcoholic, and a known prostitute. She was discovered lying in a pool of blood, on her back, her hands by her sides, her legs apart and with her clothes turned up to leave her lower body and legs exposed. She had been there since at least since 3.30 a.m. when Alfred Crow, a cab driver returning home, had seen the body – but had assumed that it was just a vagrant sleeping rough – but not before 2 a.m. when another resident passed the same spot and observed nothing. Detective Inspector Edmund Reid of H Division (who also investigated the Emma Smith,

Mary Kelly, and Alice McKenzie murders – see pages 62, 44, and 76 respectively) took statements from residents, but none could provide any useful information to advance the enquiry. In fact, nobody interviewed recognised Martha as being a resident in the building, which did not have a reputation of being used for prostitution. It was later revealed that Martha had, up until a few weeks before her death, been living at No. 4 Star Place in Commercial Road so it is not clear why she should be found here in the first place.

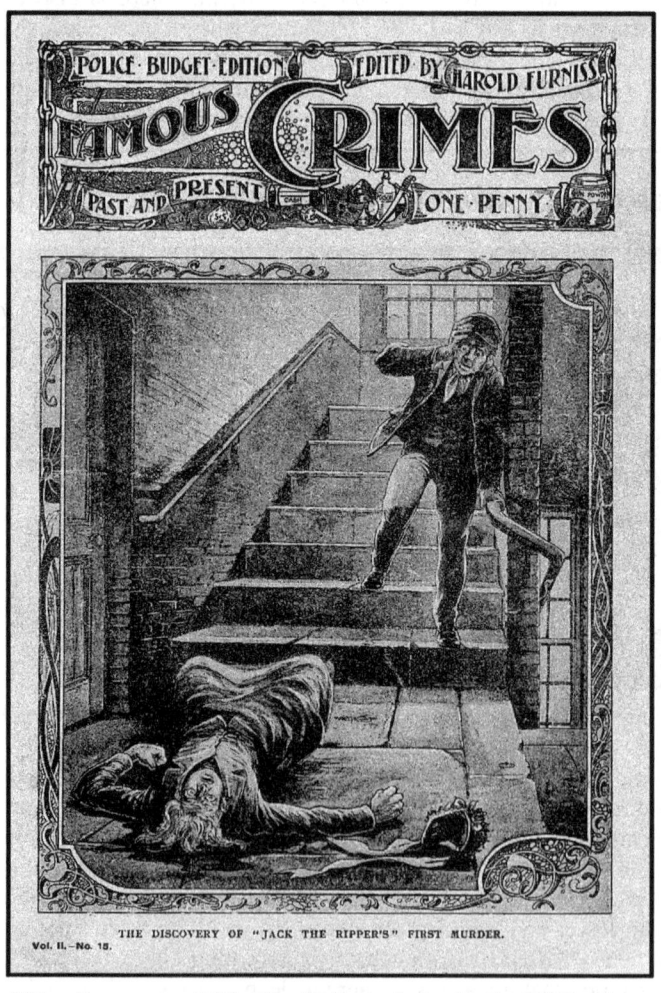

[The discovery of Martha Tabram's body. In 1903, when *Famous Crimes Past and Present* was published, she still was widely considered as being the first victim of Jack the Ripper]

The Genesis of Jack the Ripper?

The doctor who attended (Timothy Killeen) examined the corpse and found no fewer than 39 stab wounds. Despite the obvious assumption from the body position that she had been engaged in sexual intercourse, Dr. Killeen found no evidence of this activity, though there was a great deal of blood between her legs. The post-mortem showed that among the stab wounds 5 were to the left lung, 2 to the right lung, 5 to the liver, 2 to the spleen, 6 to the stomach, and a fatal one to the heart. It appeared that two different weapons had been used, one akin to a common knife (even a pen knife) while the other would be more like a dagger or bayonet (such as might be carried by a soldier).

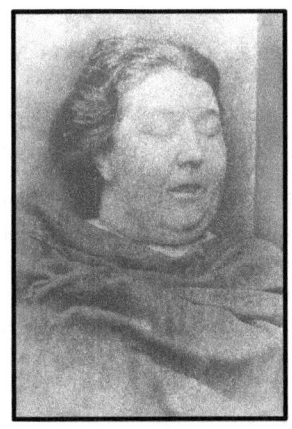

[Mortuary photograph of Martha Tabram]

A suspect, or rather a whole regiment of suspects, was soon to come to light, since, at 2 a.m. on the day in question, Police Constable Thomas Barrett, while on his beat, reported speaking with a soldier in George Yard close to George Yard Buildings. The soldier said that he was waiting for a mate who had 'gone away with a girl'. Barrett thought nothing of it at the time, but that soldier who was with the 'girl' was now the prime suspect. Barrett described the soldier he spoke to as being a Grenadier Guard (probably incorrectly), in his early to mid-twenties, of medium height, dark hair, with a small dark brown moustache turned up at the ends. He sported a good conduct badge but was without any medals.

In addition, another prostitute and friend of Tabram's, Mary Connelly (also known as Pearly Poll), came forward stating that she and Martha had been in the company of two soldiers up until just before midnight. She was able to identify one of the men as being a corporal, but that was the soldier that she had gone off with herself in the direction of Angel Court.

Hence it is likely that the private that Barrett spoke to in George Yard was, in fact, the murderer on his way back to barracks who happened to come across the policeman, and thinking on his feet made up the story about waiting for his mate. He might well have worn medals, which he quickly hid in a pocket since he knew that they could easily be used to identify him later.

Investigations revealed that Martha Tabram was married to Henry Tabram who resided in East Greenwich, but the two had been estranged for over a dozen years. They had had 2 sons together (Frederick and Charles). Since that time, she had been living on and off with a carpenter named Henry Turner (and hence in some references she is referred to as Martha Turner).

Reid and Barrett went to the Tower of London to make enquiries on the 7th August. The following day a parade of all privates and corporals that were on leave at the time of the murder was held. Barrett identified a private (who was wearing medals), but when asked to identify the soldier a second time he chose a different guardsman. It seems that Barrett may have identified the correct soldier first time, but was then swayed by the medals he was wearing and so picked another soldier without medals the second time around. The 2 soldiers were questioned, but then dismissed. Barrett made a return visit on the 9th August and interviewed a Corporal Benjiman who had been absent without leave, but he had an alibi in Kingston upon Thames. Three days later another parade was held for Connelly (who was elusive/had gone into hiding since the murder). She pronounced that the uniforms were wrong – the men she and Martha had been with had white bands around their caps, which are only worn by the Coldstream Guards who resided not at the Tower of London, but at Wellington Barracks near Buckingham Palace.

An inspection of the soldiers at Wellington Barracks by Connelly proved unsatisfactory as although she was able to positively identify two privates (George and Skipper) both of them had solid alibis. This also contradicted her previous evidence that one of the men was a corporal. The question must be asked as to just how accurate was her original statement.

In the end a verdict of 'wilful murder by person or persons unknown' was returned. It seems clear that Reid was on the right track in suspecting the murderer to be a soldier, and might even have interviewed the killer, but was hindered in his investigation by his two witnesses, one of whom being a policeman, should have been a much better observer.

The question remains, if Martha was not a resident in George Yard Buildings what was she doing there on the first-floor landing? Maybe she was led there by the mystery soldier, or maybe she was with a different client who was a resident and it was he who murdered her in his room before carrying the body out onto the landing? It should also be pointed out that the entrance arch had an iron gate, which at the time of the murder would surely have been closed and locked, so how did Martha get past the gate unless she was with a resident, or living there herself?

Whether Martha was the first Jack the Ripper victim will never be known. It is possible, given that the soldier was with Martha around midnight, and that she was supposedly still alive at 2 a.m. i.e. after the soldier, she had time to find another client (who may/may not also have been a soldier). Against this idea are the injuries, which although horrific, did not include cutting the throat or evisceration, both of which were to become trademarks of Jack the Ripper.

GEORGE YARD BUILDINGS AND TOYNBEE HALL

[The entrance to George Yard Buildings in 1938 (top left), the same view in 2020 (top right), and 2 recent photographs of Gunthorpe Street, which until 1912 was known as George Yard (bottom)]

George Yard Buildings in George Yard were model lodging houses (see page 42) constructed by the Metropolitan Board of Works around 1875 on the site of New Court and a former timber yard. They were close to the corner of George Yard and Wentworth Street, and had a central arch that gave access to the communal staircases (which were lit until around 11 p.m. each night). In all there were 48 dwellings in the block.

In 1889 George Yard Buildings were closed because there was now 'ample opportunity in neighbouring buildings' for tenants to find better accommodation – the other buildings in question being the vast blocks in Goulston Street and Wentworth Street. However, the real reason was probably that the unlet flats amounted to a loss in rent of around £60 per annum. By the following year George Yard Buildings had been converted into Balliol House to serve as a residence for students working from Toynbee Hall (named after the social philosopher Arnold Toynbee), which had opened in Commercial Road in 1884 with an aim 'to educate citizens in the knowledge of one another, to provide teaching for those willing to learn, and recreation to those who are weary'. In essence it was a radical vision in which a place was created for future leaders to live and work as volunteers in the East End, bringing them face to face with poverty, and giving them the opportunity to develop practical solutions that they could take with them into national life. Clement Atlee and William Beveridge were two such individuals who came to Toynbee Hall as young men.

[Concert in the quadrangle of Toynbee Hall, circa 1900]

Balliol House along with Wadham House (a former mothers' meeting room that in 1891 was altered to become a common room) formed a sort of secondary quadrangle, with a tennis court, behind Toynbee Hall. A dining hall was added to the rear of Balliol House, but student numbers fell as most preferred to commute from the more congenial areas of London, rather than reside in the East End. Consequently, Balliol House closed in 1913. The building was renamed Charles Booth House (after the Victorian social reformer who performed innovative philanthropic studies on the working-classes in London) and was converted into offices for the Charity Organisation Society and various other childrens' charities. It was demolished in 1973 to make way for Sunley House (named after the property developer and philanthropist Bernard Sunley), which incorporated an underground car park, 18 flats for the intellectually disabled, an office, and 2 activity rooms. This building was also demolished in 2016 and replaced by a block of flats named Broadway as part of a comprehensive redevelopment of Toynbee Hall and London Square. The George Yard Buildings were not the only thing to have a change of name for in 1912 George Yard itself became Gunthorpe Street.

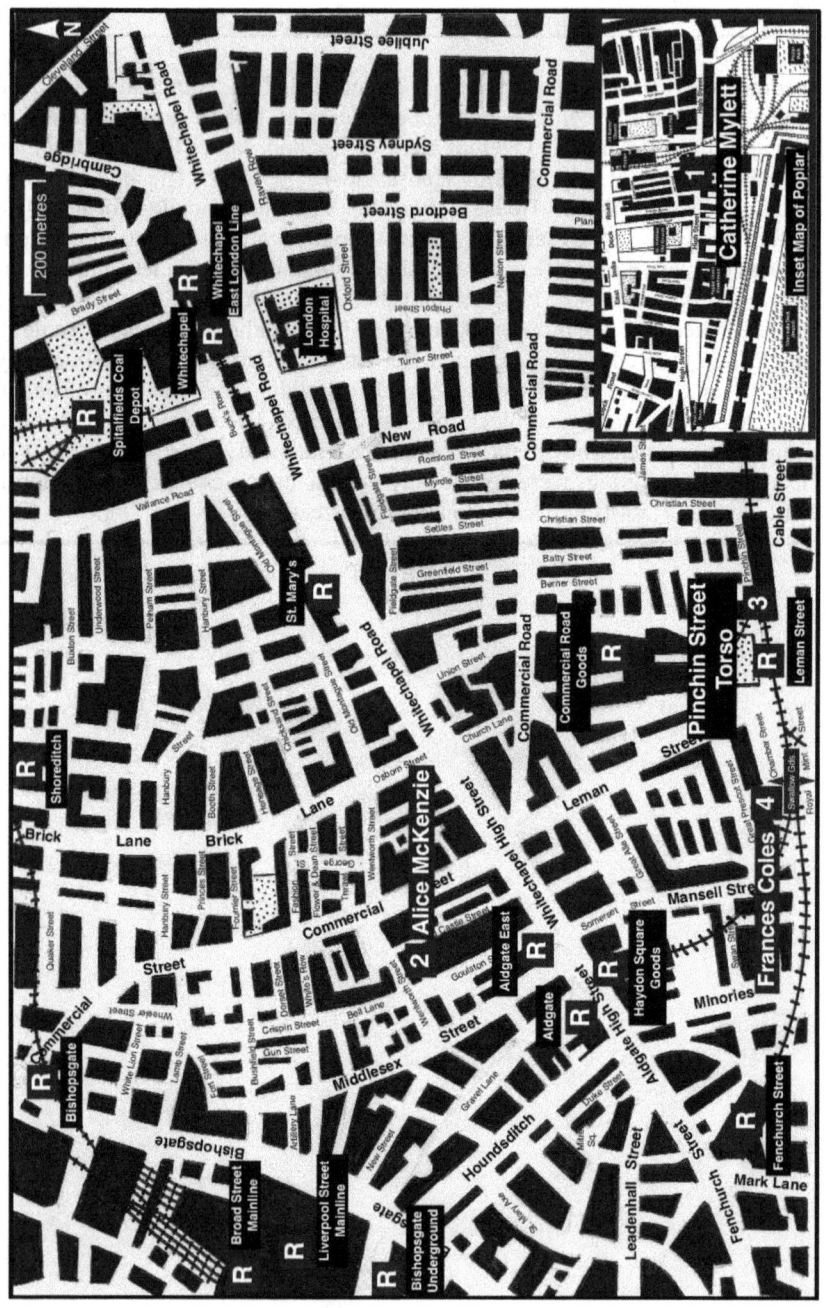

[1888 street map of the 'Return' Jack the Ripper Murders (including insert map of Poplar which is approx. 4,000 metres from Aldgate East station travelling east along Commercial Road which becomes East India Dock Road)]

THE RETURN OF JACK THE RIPPER?

Although the death of Mary Kelly in November 1888 marks the last of the canonical 5 Jack the Ripper murders that did not mean that the streets of the East End were now safe at night. Presented here are another 4 horrific East End murders that took place between December 1888 and November 1891, each of which has at some time been attributed to the possible continuing work of Jack the Ripper.

CATHERINE MYLETT (THURSDAY 20TH DECEMBER 1888)

[*The Police Illustrated News* drawings of the Catherine Mylett killing]

Catherine Mylett was also known by a number of names including Rose Mylett, Catherine Milllett, Catherine Mellett, 'Drunken Lizzie' Davis, and 'Fair Alice' Downey. She was born on the 8th December 1859, and was married until 1888 to an upholsterer called Davis by whom she had a daughter (Florence) in 1880. Catherine had lived in a variety of lodging houses, was known as a prostitute, and also an alcoholic.

At 2.30 a.m. on the 20th December 1888 she was spotted outside The George Tavern in Commercial Road in the company of two men, who might well have been the same two men she had been seen talking with 6 hours earlier in Poplar High Street. It was at 4.15 a.m. that Police Sergeant Robert Golding found her body in Clarke's Yard (a builder's merchant) between No. 184 and No. 186 Poplar High Street. The body was on its left side with the left leg drawn up, and the right leg stretched out. Some say this was reminiscent of a Jack the Ripper killing, albeit without any signs of injury, but could equally have been an attempt by somebody to place the body in the recovery position.

[The George Tavern, now demolished, around 2008 (left) and the location of where Clarke's Yard once stood in Poplar High Street in 2020 (right)]

It was only much later under the closer examination of a post-mortem (performed by Dr. Matthew Brownfield) that a faint mark, such as might be made by a cord being pulled tight, around the neck from the spine to the left ear suggested strangulation. Blood was oozing from the nostrils and there were impressions of the thumbs, middle, and index fingers of someone plainly visible on each side of the neck. Catherine was attacked from behind, and had recently ingested food (meat and potatoes). However, Dr. Robert Anderson who searched the area in which the body was found reported that there was no sign of a struggle (i.e. nothing had been strewn about, no clothing had been ripped or torn, there were no scratches on the body, and no second set of footprints to be seen on the soft ground in the yard). In his opinion the body 'lay naturally'.

Not surprisingly, it was Anderson's version that the police preferred since it meant far less paperwork, and no possibility of a murder hunt. To be certain Dr. Anderson wanted another professional opinion from a Dr. Thomas Bond in Westminster, but his request was intercepted by Bond's assistant who, along with the Senior Police Surgeon, then went and examined the body for themselves. They agreed on the original diagnosis of strangulation.

Later, Dr. Bond was to examine the corpse, but he found no trace of strangulation as the faint marks had by now disappeared. Normally there would be additional secondary signs of strangulation, such as a protruding tongue or clenched fists, but these too were missing. He put forward the theory that she had merely collapsed due to drink and choked to death by her stiff velvet collar. Dr. Bond would also be the centre of a professional disagreement in the Alice McKenzie murder (see page 77), and involved with the Catherine Eddowes and Mary Kelly investigations (see pages 37 and 48 respectively).

The Return of Jack the Ripper?

At the inquest, presided over by Wynne Baxter, the police were unhappy with the report submitted by Dr. Brownfield, but Baxter wanted nothing to do with this 'nonsense ... (of) death caused by natural causes'. He also pointed out that Dr. Bond did not see the body until 5 days after death. Baxter's view prevailed with the verdict being 'wilful murder by persons or persons unknown'. Despite this the police refused to take any further action deeming it to be a waste of resources.

POPLAR

[St. Mattias Old Church (left), and almshouses (right) – both were built by the East India Company which dominated Poplar]

Poplar only became a parish in 1817, and is thought to take its name from the trees (*Populus canescens* and *Populus nigra*) that flourished in the marshy ground nearby. In medieval times it was a fishing village centred around the High Street, but from the time of King Henry VIII it could accommodate large ocean-going ships.

In time this attracted the East India Company who had many of its ships constructed in Blackwall. In Poplar they built almshouses and a chapel (St. Matthias Old Church which still stands in Poplar High Street). By the turn of the 19th century the population was around 4,500, but Poplar was to expand rapidly with the opening of the East and West India Docks, which were linked to it by both the East India Dock Road and Commercial Road. Between the 1830s and 1850s the area north of East India Dock Road (Poplar Fields) became Poplar New Town. It was an area of both skilled and unskilled labour reaching a population of 55,000 in 1881. By 1930 Poplar was the poorest borough in London, and it declined further during World War II as around half the properties were damaged/destroyed by German bombing.

This, however, this did provide an opportunity for redevelopment, though despite all efforts and some regeneration along the riverside it still remains an area of high unemployment, poor housing, and social depravation.

ALICE MCKENZIE (WEDNESDAY 17TH JULY 1889)

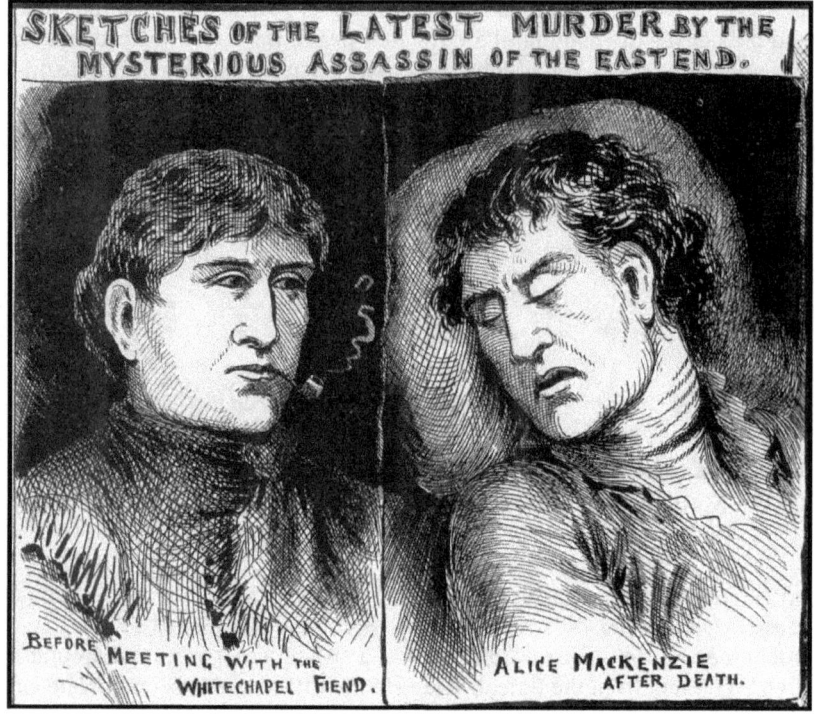

[Sketches of Alice McKenzie from *The Illustrated Police News*]

Around April 1888, John McCormack took up residence at a lodging house in Gun Street which was managed by Elizabeth Ryder. McCormack's common-law wife was Alice McKenzie (also know as Alice Bryant and 'Clay Pipe' Alice) who worked for her Jewish neighbours as a washerwoman and charwoman. She was also a prostitute, and fond of both drink and tobacco (preferably in a pipe and hence her nickname).

On the 16th July 1889 McCormack returned home from work at approximately 4 p.m. and gave Alice 1s. 8d. to pay the rent plus a further 1s. for household expenses. Alice never paid the rent, but went with a blind boy called George Dixon (who was also a resident at the lodging) to the Royal Cambridge Music Hall. Afterwards she returned home, and then left again around 8.30 p.m. when Ryder says she saw (a drunken) Alice depart following an argument with McCormack. This statement contradicts that of McCormack who said that he did not see Alice after 4 p.m. that day.

The Return of Jack the Ripper?

[The discovery of the body by Police Constable Andrews (left), and the mortuary photograph of Alice McKenzie (right)]

Later that evening, just before midnight, Alice was spotted in the vicinity of Flower and Dean Street and Brick Lane (see page 64). At 12.45 a.m. it began to rain and 5 minutes later Police Constable Walter Andrews, on his beat, entered Castle Alley (just off Whitechapel High Street between Nos. 122 and 125). Close to a lamp post he discovered Alice's body with two stab wounds to the left side of her neck. Her skirt had been lifted and her abdomen mutilated. The body was not there at 12.20 a.m. when Andrews had last passed the spot, and a resident in Castle Alley who was reading in bed at the time heard nothing unusual until Andrews blew his whistle to summon assistance.

Shortly after 1.00 a.m. both Detective Inspector Edmund Reid (who had also been involved in the Emma Smith, Martha Tabram, and Mary Kelly investigations – see pages 62, 65, and 47 respectively), and Dr. George Bagster Phillips (who was involved with the Mary Kelly and Frances Coles murders – see pages 48, and 84 respectively) were at the scene. The pavement beneath the body was dry, placing the time of death after 12.45 a.m. (when it started to rain). Further examination of the corpse revealed that the cause of death was the severing of the carotid artery. In addition, there were two stab wounds to the neck, bruising on the chest, 5 bruises on the abdomen, a long cut between the left breast and navel, multiple scratches from the navel toward the genitalia, and a small cut across the *mons veneris*. Although, at first, it might look like a Jack the Ripper killing, there were differences in that the wounds were much shallower, the implement used much smaller, and it was all done by a left-handed person.

However, as with the Catherine Mylett case (see page 73) there would be a difference of opinion between the medical professionals. Phillips maintained that it was not consistent with being the work of Jack the Ripper, while Dr. Thomas

Bond (who was also involved with the Catherine Eddowes, Mary Kelly, and Catherine Mylett investigations – see pages 37, 48, and 74 respectively) who examined the body the day after the post mortem, was convinced that it was a Jack the Ripper killing. The police were not of one mind either – James Monro (the Police Commissioner who had recently replaced Sir Charles Warren and would also be involved in the Pinchin Street Torso case – see page 81) who arrived at the murder scene at 3 a.m. was inclined to believe that Jack the Ripper had returned, whereas Robert Anderson (the Assistant Police Commissioner who had been away on holiday at the time of the murder) was not. The police did place an extra 22 officers on duty the day of the murder. The inquest returned a verdict of 'murder by a person or persons unknown'.

CASTLE ALLEY

[Old Castle Street in 2020 –Alice McKenzie's body was found just past the bicycles on the left-hand side]

Castle Alley, which ran between Castle Street and Whitechapel High Street (and parallel with Goulston Street – see page 38), has changed names several times in its history. In the middle of the 18th century it was known as Moses and Aaron Alley, a name it kept until the 19th century when it became Castle

Court, and then by the middle of that century Castle Alley. At the time of Alice's murder the alley was extremely narrow (only about 18 feet wide) and was entered via a covered archway at the Whitechapel High Street end (only 3 feet wide). It was the place where tradesmen and costermongers would store their carts and barrows.

[The Wash Houses façade dating from 1846 has been preserved and incorporated into the new library building]

The west side had warehouses and the back of the Whitechapel Wash Houses, while on the east side there were a number of smaller properties. At the far end there was a sharp bend and the Old Castle Street Board School. The alley was only around 180 yards long, and was described by the press as being 'one of the lowest quarters in the whole of East London'. It apparently had an 'evil reputation' compounded by 'the absence of any inhabitants in the immediate vicinity'. Despite there being 3 lamp posts it was said that the alley still afforded 'ample cover and secrecy for crime and violence'. Alice was lying in a spot between two chained-up barrows outside the premises of a builders, Messrs. King and Sons. In 1890 the east side of the alley at the Whitechapel High Street end was demolished to make it wider, and it was widened again in 1908. By 1916 it had become part of Old Castle Street, and in 1930 the school was replaced by a block of flats (Herbert House). During World War II there was damage on the eastern side which led to the redevelopment of the area and the building of the New Holland estate. Finally, the wash houses became part of the London Metropolitan University's Women's Library opened in 2002.

THE PINCHIN STREET TORSO (TUESDAY 10ᵀᴴ SEPTEMBER 1889)

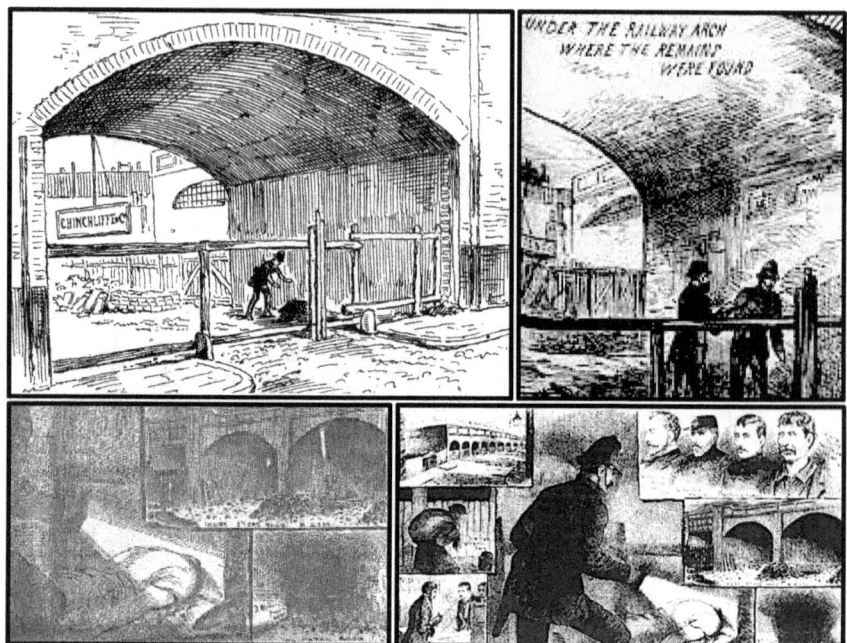

[Various drawings concerning the Pinchin Street
murder from the popular press of the time]

At 5.20 a.m. on the 10th September 1889, Police Constable William Pennett found a headless torso of a woman (covered in an old chemise) under a railway arch at Pinchin Street. The railway arch in question was that of the London & Blackwall Railway.

There was extensive bruising to the back, hip, and arm indicating that the female victim, whom it was estimated was between 30 and 40-years of age, had been severely beaten prior to death. The abdomen was mutilated, but the genitalia were not touched. No other body parts were found in the area, and it was assumed from this, and the lack of blood, that the victim was murdered elsewhere and subsequently dumped in Pinchin Street. If it weren't for the fact that she was under the arch it would have been a reasonable hypothesis to say that she had been thrown from the railway tracks above, albeit there were few trains at that time of day. Certainly, she was not there 20 minutes earlier when Pennett had last passed the spot.

The Return of Jack the Ripper?

[Pinchin Street then (left), and in 2020 (right) – the torso was found under the first bricked up arch (with 4 windows) to the right of the picture]

A closer inspection of the body revealed that there was blood inside the torso, a sign that death was not from the cutting of the throat. It was also determined that the victim was killed between 24 and 36 hours prior to the finding of the body. The killing was certainly a gruesome one and in the right location to be the work of Jack the Ripper. However, given that the mutilations did not match the type of injuries inflicted to other Jack the Ripper victims, and that they might have been performed anywhere in London, it is unlikely that this murder can be attributed to him (despite the speculation of some newspaper reports at the time). As Chief Commissioner James Monro (who was involved in the Alice McKenzie murder – see page 78) put it, 'there was no sign of frenzied mutilation of the body, but of deliberate and skilful dismemberment with a view to removal' of limbs.

It is quite possible that this murder was connected with a series of similar killings that Scotland Yard were already investigating. In fact, this was remarked upon by Assistant Chief Constable Sir Melville Macnaghten who wrote that 'the stomach was split up by a cut, and the head and legs had been severed in a manner identical with that of a woman whose remains were discovered in the Thames, in Battersea Park, and along the Chelsea Embankment (i.e. in two locations, with more to follow) on 4th June of the same year; and these murders had no connection whatever with the Whitechapel horrors. The Rainham mystery in 1887, and the Whitehall mystery (when portions of a woman's body were found under what is now New Scotland Yard) in 1888 were of a similar type to the Thames and Pinchin Street crimes'. The bodies in question were part of what became known as the Thames Torso Murders investigation that took place between 1887 and 1889. The case included at least 4 deaths (only one body was identified – a homeless prostitute from Chelsea called Elizabeth Jackson) and was never solved.

The identity of the Pinchin Street torso was also never discovered, so on the 5th October 1889 the remains were laid to rest in the East London Cemetery in

Plaistow. The coffin carried a plate which simply read 'This case contains the body of a woman (unknown) found in Pinchin Street St. Georges-in-the-East 10th Septr./89'.

PINCHIN STREET

[The curve of the railway spur at Pinchin Street]

Pinchin Street runs east to west from Christian Street to Back Church Lane, and was originally known as Rope Walk. The north side was lined with run-down houses while the south side was made up of arches supporting the London & Blackwall Railway. In fact, Pinchin Street follows a spur from the mainline to Fenchurch Street which went to warehouses for the London, Tilbury & Southend Railway at Commercial Road. The area was densely crowded with many Germans, Polish and Russians. It was extensively bombed during World War II necessitating a redevelopment, so today there is some 1950s housing and the railway arches (albeit for a long since disused section of the railway), which have been bricked up to form a variety of businesses and garage space.

FRANCES COLES (FRIDAY 13TH NOVEMBER 1891)

[*The Illustrated Police News* sketches of the Frances Coles murder]

On Friday 13th November 1891 Police Constable Ernest Thompson entering the area from Chamber Street, found the body of Frances Coles (sometimes Cole in the literature) under a railway arch at Swallow Gardens (which at that time was little more than an alleyway running under the railway line). It was 2.15 a.m. and Thompson was quite sure that the body was not there when he had passed the same spot on his beat 15 minutes earlier. He reported having heard footsteps during his approach, so he might well have interrupted the murderer but, following correct police procedure, he stayed with the body and did not attempt to investigate the sound. On examination he observed that Coles was lying in a pool of blood with her throat cut from ear to ear. He called for assistance by blowing his whistle, and very soon he had been joined by Police Constables Frederick Hyde, Hinton, and George Elliott (the latter having been on plain-clothes duty in Royal Mint Street).

Together they assessed the body further, and found, unbelievably, that there was still a faint pulse, though by the time Dr. Frederick Oxley arrived (who Hyde fetched) Coles was dead. Meanwhile Hinton had gone to get a senior police officer (Detective Inspector James Flanagan) who on arrival ordered that the crime scene be left untouched, while officers were directed to search the area and question anybody on the streets at the time. The Divisional Police Surgeon, Dr. Bagster Philips (who had been involved with Mary Kelly, and Alice McKenzie murders – see pages 48, and 77 respectively) stated that although horrific, the lack of mutilation was not consistent with it being the work of Jack the Ripper. At this point in the investigation the name of the victim was not known – this had to wait until the following evening (Valentine's Day) when James Coles (father), who was in a Bermondsey workhouse, and Mary Coles (sister), who lived in Kingsland, were able to identify the body as that of Frances Coles.

[Mortuary photograph of Frances Coles (left) and Swallow Street as featured in *The Penny Illustrated Paper* (right)]

Little is known about Frances except that she was a prostitute who at one time had worked in the Minories as a labeller of bottles at a wholesale chemists, and had until recently lodged in Thrawl Street, but had left with rent in arrears. Just a few hours before her murder she had returned to Thrawl Street and asked her former landlady, Mrs. Hague, to let her come back if she were able to clear her debts. On questioning, Mrs. Hague said that she had later seen Frances in a public house in Montague Street with a man of fair complexion, and sporting a moustache. It did not take the police long to find the man in question, James Sadler, and from his statement to the police the last couple of days of Coles' life became clearer.

Sadler was a 53-year old merchant seaman and fireman on the *Fez* and had known Frances (in the capacity of a client) since February that year. Two days prior to the murder they had visited the Princess Alice public house, and then spent the night together at Spitafields Chambers (a common lodging house). They were still together the following day, and seemed to go on a pub crawl of the East End for most of it. That evening, a drunk Frances purchased a black crepe hat from a milliners at No. 25 Nottingham Street, paying for her purchase with 2s. 6d. which Sadler had given her. Sadler was still with her, though he did not enter the shop. Later that evening while walking together in Thrawl Street, Sadler was attacked and robbed of his watch and money by two men and a woman in a red shawl. It was after this that they went their separate ways since Sadler was angry that Coles did not assist him during the attack (and it has even been suggested that she might have instigated it in the first place). However, they met again at the lodging house where they had spent the previous night, but now, having no money to pay for the accommodation they both had to leave. Sadler left first having been cleaned up by the night watchman. Coles left later (after midnight) once she came around from passing out from drink in the kitchen. At around 1.45 a.m. she was in the company of another prostitute, Ellen Callana, in Commercial Street, and was solicited by 'a violent man in a cheese cutter hat'. Whereas Ellen refused the client and received a black eye from him, Frances did not and went off with him in the direction of Minories.

Meanwhile Sadler headed back to his ship, but became involved in a fight with a group of dockworkers – it just wasn't his night! He was next seen on the pavement outside the Royal Mint by a patrolling police officer. He was described as being 'drunk and bloodied'. He was probably in no fit state to commit a murder, though he was certainly in the vicinity at the time Coles was murdered, but then so was 'cheese cutter hat'.

The police arrested Sadler and questioned him at the Leman Street police station for around 40 hours. On the night of Sunday 15th February he was formally charged with the murder. The potentially damning fact that came to light was that, on the day of the murder, Sadler had sold his knife to one Donald Campbell, possibly to get rid of it. Campbell had subsequently sold it on to a marine stores dealer.

At the inquest it appeared very likely that Sadler would be found guilty, until it was revealed that his knife was so blunt that it would be unable to cut a throat in the manner observed. As to the assertion that he was Jack the Ripper, this was easy to disprove since Sadler was at sea when some of the murders took place. Even so Sadler had to make a further court appearance before a magistrate on the 3rd March 1891 in order to learn that 'no further evidence should now be offered against the accused'. As he left the court a free man, he was cheered by a large crowd who had been convinced of his innocence all along. It seems clear that it was 'cheese cutter hat' that the police should have concentrated on finding. The murderer was never found, though many at Scotland Yard were of the opinion that Sadler was guilty. Indeed, if Sadler had not had proper legal representation (which in his case was paid for by the Seaman's Union) the outcome might well have been very different.

SWALLOW GARDENS

[Chamber Street clearly showing the railway spur from the mainline into Fenchurch Street to Haydon Square – Swallow Gardens was the filled-in arch immediately to the left of the iron pillar]

Swallow Gardens, where Frances Coles was found, was originally on the site of some gardens and/or orchards which had been laid out north of Rosemary Lane (now Royal Mint Street) and to the south of Chamber Street (which runs between Leman Street and Mansell Street). By the mid-18th century there were houses here, but the major change came when the London & Blackwall Railway started construction in 1836. The line between Minories and Blackwall via Stepney was opened in 1840. It ran on ropes and gravity initially, due to the likelihood of cinders from any steam boiler setting fire to the wooden tenements close to the elevated track.

Today that railway forms part of the line between Fenchurch Street, Tilbury and Southend-on-Sea (with the site of the long gone Minories depot being occupied by Tower Gateway station on the Docklands Light Railway). As a consequence Swallow Street became an alleyway running through a railway arch connecting Royal Mint Street and Chamber Street. That alleyway is also long gone as all the railway arches in the area have been blocked off and converted into lock-ups and small businesses.

[Swallow Gardens – the arch next to the building – from Royal Mint Street with a train passing overhead (top), and the office space that was once Swallow Gardens as accessed from Chamber Street (Bottom)]

🔍 CLUES AND 🐟 RED HERRINGS

'There is nothing more deceptive than an obvious fact.'
(Sherlock Holmes, *The Boscombe Valley Mystery*)

For as long as there has been interest in Jack the Ripper so people have been putting forward their own theories. Presented here are some of the most common statements that have been cited as clues, along with an assessment as to their validity, for what may at first seem to be a clue may later transpire to be a red herring, or even both leading to an entirely different conclusion.

🔍 🐟 **The Goulston Street graffito** – Beyond any other possible clue the words, 'The Juwes are The men That Will not be Blamed for nothing' written in chalk on the wall in Goulston Street (see page 38) above where the missing fragment of apron belonging to Catherine Eddowes was found has been the object of intense speculation. Was it written by Jack the Ripper? Why was it removed before being photographed?

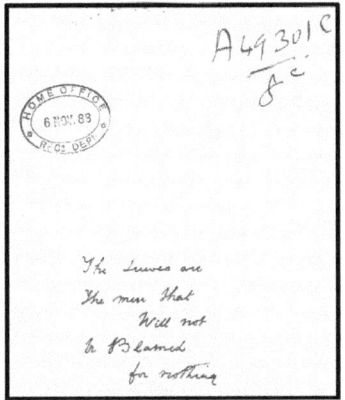

[Copy of the graffito as sent by Sir Charles Warren in a report to the Home Office]

It is the view of this author that it is almost certainly a red herring for there is no good reason as to why Jack the Ripper should just happen to be carrying a piece of chalk with him that evening, let alone feel the need to write a message on a wall having just performed 2 gruesome murders, and needing upmost to make an escape from an area soon to be swarming with police. He certainly did not leave any such messages close to any of his other victims. The only reason that the graffito is considered at all is because the missing fragment of apron belonging to Catherine Eddowes was found at the same location.

It could be that Jack the Ripper, while exiting the area, saw the graffito and decided to add the apron at the base in an effort to mislead the police (see page 110). The anti-Jewish sentiment of the graffito may have prompted this action if it is considered that in the earlier Elizabeth Stride murder that there was a report of Jack the Ripper shouting the word 'Lipski' (see page 32) at a passerby. However, in one theory (see page 94) the graffito does reveal the identity of Jack the Ripper.

The most likely reason for its removal was exactly as stated by Sir Charles Warren in his letter to the Home Office on the 6th November 1888, 'The most pressing question at that moment was some writing on the wall in Goulston Street evidently written with the intention of inflaming the public mind against the Jews, and which Mr. Arnold with a view to prevent serious disorder proposed to obliterate, and had sent down an Inspector with a sponge for that purpose telling him to await his arrival ... it was just getting light, the public would be in the streets in a few minutes, in a neighbourhood very much crowded on Sunday mornings by Jewish vendors and Christian purchasers from all parts of London ... A discussion took place whether the writing could be left or covered up or otherwise or whether any portion of it could be left for an hour until it could be photographed ... I considered it desirable to obliterate the writing at once, having taken a copy ...'. He was factually correct for examination of an 1899 map of the Jewish East End reveals that the immediate area around Goulston Street had a Jewish population in excess of 95%.

The City of London – Again a lot is made by some 'Ripperologists' that the murder of Catherine Eddowes did not take place in the East End but within the City of London.

This must be another red herring for surely Jack the Ripper would not know, or care, that he had strayed 50 metres over the official boundary line. However, this author believes it does provide a vital clue as to where Jack the Ripper was heading on the night of the 'double event' (see page 109).

[City boundary mark]

Since the late 1960s every entry point into the City of London is 'guarded' by a dragon boundary mark. In essence each of the 13 dragons is a cast iron statue of a dragon on a metal or stone plinth. The dragons are painted silver, with details of their wings and tongue picked out in red. The dragon stands on one rear leg, the other lifted against a shield, with the right foreleg raised and the left foreleg holding the shield which bears the City of London coat of arms painted in white and red. The stance is the equivalent of the rampant heraldic attitude of the supporters of the City's arms. They are, in fact, smaller copies of two such sculptures that in 1849 were mounted above the entrance to the Coal Exchange in Lower Thames Street.

Expertise – this is a contentious subject for at the time the scientific opinions differed as to whether Jack the Ripper had some sort of anatomical/butchery knowledge or not. Clearly, Dr. Thomas Bond, Dr. William

Saunders, and Dr. Bagster Phillips were all of the opinion that Jack the Ripper possessed no such knowledge (see pages 37 and 48) whereas reports of the earlier murders (see pages 25 and 37) did suggest such skills and led to the hunt for 'Leather Apron'. This author maintains that most people would be hard-pressed to locate a kidney within a corpse let alone remove it, but against this is one of the points made by Bond *et al* in that the cuts were jagged i.e. not smooth such as a surgeon or butcher might make, thus indicating a lack of skill. However, it is argued here that if you placed a butcher on a pavement in the wet and cold, with no or little light to work by, and gave them just a couple of minutes to complete the operation with the aid of a single 6 inch blade, then the result might well be similar to that achieved by Jack the Ripper.

► **All the victims were 'unfortunate women'** – this is certainly a red herring for Whitechapel had around 5,000 prostitutes, and almost every woman out on the streets at the times in question would have been a prostitute looking for a client. Hence, it should be no surprise that all the Jack the Ripper victims were 'unfortunate women'. It does, however, show that there was a certain randomness to his killings.

► **All the victims were drinkers** – again this is a red herring since the majority of prostitutes were chronic alcoholics. It is also likely that Jack the Ripper would seek out such persons as they would be easier to over power. It should be pointed out that each of the women was seen at one or more public houses just prior to their deaths (except Catherine Eddowes who had been in a cell at Bishopsgate police station getting sober). This should be expected since the public houses were effectively the women's 'offices' where they might meet their next client, especially on evenings when it was raining (as it was on several of the nights in question). This implies that to choose his next victim, or to fuel his desires, that Jack the Ripper might have been in the same public houses on the evenings in question, and then followed his intended victims when they left. However, there is no police evidence to suggest that a man had been seen either inside, or keeping watch outside, any of the public houses in question at the times of the murders.

► **Flowers** – it has been noted that several of the victims had a connection to flowers and/or a new piece of clothing. Polly Nichols was wearing a new black straw bonnet, Annie Chapman used to sell flowers, Elizabeth Stride was wearing a red rose posy, and Catherine Eddowes was wearing a skirt with a design of lilies. At best it could have been that the sight of flowers and/or new clothing would act as an initial attraction for Jack the Ripper when choosing his next victim.

► **The surname Kelly** – Various 'Ripperologists' have tried to make a case for Jack the Ripper seeking out a certain woman with the surname Kelly, and to this end they cite the deaths of Catherine Eddowes, who also went by the name of

Catherine Kelly (after her current partner John Kelly), and Mary Kelly, the final victim. However, this would appear to be a non-starter as a theory since, surely, he would not have known the names of his victims beforehand?

➤ **Possession** – There have been various theories as to why Jack the Ripper wanted to keep organs from his victims. Mostly the reason is a simple one in that serial killers often want a souvenir/trophy of their victim since it helps the murderer prolong, even nourish, their fantasy of the crime. Usually this takes the form of some object such as a piece of clothing or jewellery, but in more sadistic and extreme cases actual body parts may be kept. In some ways it gives the killer a sense of ownership of that person as a whole – an accomplishment that they feel good about. It is actually quite a common occurrence so must be considered a red herring here as it must have been pretty obvious to all by the Autumn of 1888 that London had a serial killer at large.

➤ **Age of the victims** – the fact that the first 4 women were middle-aged (for the time) and the final victim, Mary Kelly, was only 25-years old has been cited as a clue. Some 'Ripperologists' believe that this points to the last murder as not being done by Jack the Ripper. This author believes that Jack the Ripper just 'took what was on offer', irrespective of their age. It should also be remembered that on the night of the Mary Kelly killing that the weather had been atrocious with heavy rain. Hence, most prostitutes would be either in the public houses if still looking for clients, or at their residence, but certainly not walking the streets.

➤ **'Dear Boss' Letters** – The various letters purportedly sent by Jack the Ripper have already been considered (see pages 26, and 39) and dismissed as being hoaxes, written in the main to increase newspaper circulation.

➤ **'Lipski'** – The word shouted by Jack the Ripper to a stranger in the street just prior to the Elizabeth Stride murder is most likely a red herring (see page 32).

[Was this the Ripper?]

In his statement to the police Israel Schwartz said that he saw a woman, later identified as Elizabeth Stride, being assaulted in Berner Street with the attacker shouting out the word 'Lipski'. Police had to judge whether this was the surname of Jack the Ripper, or was just being used as an ethnic slur against Jews in general. Although there were several Lipskis living in the immediate area, upon investigation the police concluded upon the latter explanation.

SUSPECTS ASSEMBLE

'How dangerous it always is to reason from insufficient data.'
(Sherlock Holmes, *The Adventure of the Speckled Band*)

[There was no shortage of suspects according to the press]

Below alphabetically are a selection of the suspects most featured in the media at the time and subsequently, along with a star rating (on a scale from 1 to 5) of how damning the evidence against each of them is perceived to be.

JOSEPH BARNETT ★★★

It is speculated that Barnett, who was Mary Kelly's lover (see page 45), so hated the thought of her turning to prostitution after he had lost his job as a fish porter at Billingsgate (where he undoubtedly was proficient with a knife), that he turned to murdering prostitutes to frighten his girlfriend away from that trade. Moreover he had recently argued with Mary, and was at the time of her murder separated from her.

It is also true that he had been with her at home earlier in the evening on the night of her death, and that Mary had been in the presence of another woman (possibly also a prostitute). In addition, Mary had been known to periodically share her accommodation with other prostitutes out of pity for them – something that must have infuriated Barnett. On this basis he certainly had motive, means (it is conjectured that he still retained a key to Kelly's lodgings which he later claimed had been lost for some weeks) and probably opportunity. After the murder Barnett was interviewed for 4 hours by Detective Inspector Abberline, and his clothes were examined for blood stains. He was not called upon again and seemed to satisfy the police that he was at his lodging house all evening once he left Mary, though it is possible that he could have slipped out unnoticed to commit the deed. If he was Jack the Ripper he had the advantage that being a boyfriend of a prostitute he was probably known to, and trusted by, the other victims. Further there was circumstantial evidence since after Annie Chapman's death (see page 21), an envelope that belonged to Barnett was found in the yard at Hanbury Street – a coincidence indeed.

The Goulston Street graffito (see page 38) might even have been written by Barnett and contained a coded message for Mary. It has never been established what the definitive version of the graffito was since slightly different versions exist. Consider that written down by Sir Charles Warren:

> 'The **J**uwes are
> The men that
> Will not
> be **B**lamed
> for nothing'.

It is interesting to note that apart from several of the first words of each line starting with a capital letter (as in a piece of poetry), that 'Blamed' also has a capital letter, and that when combined with the only other word with a capital letter, 'Juwes', it yields the initials 'JB' i.e. Joseph Barnett is the man who will not be blamed for nothing! Although this may all seem to point to Barnett's guilt it is very probably a case of making a theory fit selective facts, rather than having all the facts fit a theory.

DR. THOMAS NEILL CREAM ★

A very doubtful suspect, though he was certainly a serial killer. The problem is that his *modus operandi* was poison (strychnine) and his aim was always financial gain. He operated as a doctor in the United States, Canada and London where he specialised in illegal abortions. The only reason he is considered a suspect is that on the gallows on the 15th November 1892 his last words were, 'I am Jack the …' with the end of his sentence being interrupted by the noose tightening as he dropped to his death. It is likely that Cream just wanted the notoriety.

MONTAGUE DRUITT ★★

This was certainly one of 3 prime suspects at the time according to Assistant Chief Constable Melville Macnaghten. Born on the 15th August 1857, Druitt studied classics at New College, Oxford and may have also studied medicine before settling on becoming a barrister (being called to the bar in 1885). He had chambers at the Inner Temple, and to supplement his income was also an assistant schoolmaster at a prestigious school in Blackheath, a position from which he was sacked on the 1st December 1888 (reason unknown). Shortly afterwards he committed suicide by drowning.

He left a letter in which he referred to his insane mother thus, 'Since Friday I felt I was going to be like Mother and the best thing for me was to die'. His body was recovered from the Thames on the 31st December 1888. He was considered sexually insane (i.e. got erotic pleasure from ultraviolence) and had no alibi at the time of the killings, though only hours after 2 of the murders he was known to be playing cricket for his club, Blackheath. He had no connections to the East End, and it seems likely that it was a mere coincidence that the murders stopped immediately after his death.

SIR WILLIAM WITHEY GULL ★

As an extension to the theory that Prince Albert Victor was at the centre of Jack the Ripper murders (see page 100), it has been suggested that Sir William Gull acted as an accomplice (himself aided by a coachman named John Netley). Gull was an eminent physician who among other achievements was Governor of Guy's Hospital, President of the Clinical Society, Fullerian Professor of Physiology at the Royal Institution of Great Britain, and a royal physician. He did valuable research into myxoedema, Bright's disease, paraplegia and anorexia nervosa (which he named).

It is claimed that he was also a high-ranking Freemason, and it is the secretive nature of this organisation that has given rise to speculation that, acting on orders to cover up the birth of an illegitimate child of Prince Albert Victor and a Catholic prostitute, he was enticed to become Jack the Ripper to save the Royal family being subjected to blackmail. If nothing else this theory can be discounted on the basis that in 1888, Gull was 71-years old and in poor health. According to the Stephen Knight book, *Jack the Ripper: The Final Solution*, Freemasons Lord Salisbury (the Prime Minister), Sir Charles Warren, Sir Robert Anderson, and Sir William Gull conspired together to save the reputation of the Crown. However, only Sir Charles Warren was ever a Freemason according to the United Grand Lodge of England records.

AARON KOSMINSKI ★★★★

[Could either of these sketches be a likeness of Aaron Kosminski?]

Kosminski was one of 3 prime suspects at the time according to Assistant Chief Constable Melville Macnaghten, and also the favoured suspect by Assistant Commissioner Robert Anderson. In fact, Anderson wrote about Kosminski several times (without reference to him by name) saying on one occasion, 'I will only add that when the individual whom we suspected was caged in an asylum, the only person who had ever had a good view of the murderer at once identified him, but when he learned that the suspect was a fellow-Jew he declined to swear to him'. What is certain is that Kosminski was a Polish Jew living in Whitechapel who worked as a barber and had a hatred of all women, and, in particular, prostitutes. He was a paranoid schizophrenic, although in the asylum he was described as being harmless with his only misdemeanours being threatening his sister (or in some references another woman) with a knife and brandishing a chair at an asylum attendant. His English was also so poor that it is unlikely that he could persuade any of the victims into a dark alleyway. In 2014 he was identified as Jack the Ripper via DNA taken from the shawl of Catherine Eddowes, but that study has been widely criticised as having a number of mistakes and false assumptions (not least of which is that Eddowes never had such a shawl). It is also possible that it is a case of false identity since at the same time there was another Polish Jew (a bootmaker) at the same asylum who was violent and had to be restrained – he was know as Aaron Davis Cohen, or Davis Cohen though it has been speculated that he was actually Nathan Kaminsky. Hence it is possible that the police confused the two names. As with Montague Druitt (see page 95) much of the evidence relies on the fact that the atrocities stopped directly after Kosminski was taken off the streets, though this is erroneous since Kosminski was not committed until February 1891 which begs the question why he did not continue his killing spree, unless he was also responsible for the murder of Alice McKenzie (see page 76) *et al.*

JAMES MAYBRICK ✪✪

Ironically Maybrick was to be a murder victim himself, being poisoned (arsenic) most likely by his wife in May 1889. He was born in Liverpool and was a cotton trader, an enterprise that required him to spend time in both Britain and the United States. He was also known to be a womaniser, something which goes against him wanting to murder prostitutes. Maybrick was not a suspect at the time, and only became one in 1992 with the supposed discovery of his private diary (which became the bestselling book, *The Diary of Jack the Ripper*, the following year).

In it he confesses to being Jack the Ripper, but chemical analysis suggests that the diaries may not be genuine – the handwriting is certainly not representative of other samples of Maybrick's hand. However, a pocket watch discovered in 1993 with 'J. Maybrick' scratched on the inside cover, along with the words 'I am Jack' and the initials of the canonical 5 victims does seem to date from that period (or is a very clever forgery). Apart from the diary and watch there is no evidence to place him at scenes of crime.

MICHAEL OSTROG ✪

Like Montague Druitt (see page 95) and Aaron Kosminski (see page 96) he was suspected by Assistant Chief Constable Melville Macnaghten, and was also detained in an asylum as a homicidal maniac. He had no alibis at the time of the murders, but apart from that, any evidence against him seems weak. Ostrog was a Russian doctor (possibly) and a conman who had spent more than one spell in prison (and was possibly in prison in France at the time of the Jack the Ripper murders).

He did not really fit either the physical description of Jack the Ripper (too tall for one), or the psychological profile (he seemed to like women, albeit he preyed on them for money). Again it can only be coincidence that the murders stopped once Ostrog was imprisoned.

DR. ALEXANDER PEDACHENKO ★

His story is the stuff that could form the plot for a spy film. It is claimed that he was acting under the orders of the Russian secret police in an aim to discredit the Metropolitan Police, who were considered as Czarists for tolerating the presence of emigrant dissidents and anarchists in the East End. Pedachenko lived in South London with his sister, and according to this theory a friend of theirs, Levitski, was the one who wrote the Jack the Ripper letters. He had an accomplice, Miss Winberg, who would engage the prostitutes in conversation prior to Pedachenko murdering them. The killings stopped when it was perceived that his mission had been successful i.e. the resignation of Commissioner Sir Charles Warren. Pedachenko returned to Moscow where he was subsequently arrested for the murder of a woman in Petrograd, and placed in an asylum for the rest of his life. Apparently he was a barber surgeon, liked dressing in women's clothes on occasion, and was actually Vassily Konovalov (or Count Andrey Luiskovo). The source of information for this suspect comes from a document, *Great Russian Criminals*, authored by no less than Rasputin. However, there is no evidence that Pedachenko ever existed, and as with Dr. Stanley (see page 99) it is likely that he was a work of fiction perpetuated by the Russian government to confuse and misinform.

WALTER SICKERT ★

Walter Sickert is considered to be an important figure in the art world during the period of transition between Impressionism and Modernism. He was not a suspect at the time, but became one in the 1970s due to his (unhealthy) interest in Jack the Ripper – he even made a painting entitled *Jack the Ripper's Bedroom* based upon the assertion that his landlady had told him that she suspected her previous lodger to be Jack the Ripper. Another one of his works (actually a group of 4 pieces) is called *The Camden Town Murder* and shows Emily Dimmock, a part-time prostitute, who was killed in her home in St. Paul's Road, Camden.

He was implicated in Stephen Knight's book, *Jack the Ripper: The Final Solution*, as being an accomplice to Sir William Gull, and in 2002 crime novelist Patricia Cornwell in her book, *Portrait of a Killer: Jack the Ripper – Case Closed*, identified Sickert as Jack the Ripper on the basis that DNA extracted from one of Sickert's paintings matched that found on at least one of the letters sent to the police purporting to be from Jack the Ripper. The results have been called into question, not least because the letters are all widely considered to be hoaxes. The motive for the killings, away from the Royal conspiracy theory (see page 95), centre around Sickert having what is termed 'a congenital anomaly of his penis'. He died in 1942, which rather begs the question of why he stopped being a serial killer, if, indeed, he ever was one.

DR. STANLEY

At first inspection Dr. Stanley has a compelling motive, means and opportunity to be Jack the Ripper. Stanley was a cancer specialist in London and was said to have been motivated by grief and revenge following the death of his son, Herbert, from syphilis. He apparently contracted the disease from a prostitute named Mary Kelly on boat race night 1886. After tracking down and killing Mary, along with several of her friends, he fled to Buenos Aires where he was to die in 1918 from cancer, but not before making a deathbed confession. Unfortunately, no such doctor ever existed except in a 1929 novel, *The Mystery of Jack the Ripper*, by Leonard Matters.

DR. FRANCES TUMBLETY

Tumblety was a charlatan doctor born in Ireland who operated as an Indian herbalist in the States and Canada. He hated all women, especially prostitutes, and blamed his misogyny on his failed marriage to a prostitute. Among his peculiarities he collected uteruses, which he preserved in glass jars and showed to his male friends. In January 1875 Tumblety, who had been practicing in Liverpool, fled that city for London after one of his patients died. There is some (non-conclusive) evidence to suggest that he was resident in Whitechapel at the time of the Jack the Ripper murders.

Certainly, on the 7th November 1888 he was arrested on charges of gross indecency of a homosexual nature, but subsequently while on bail, fled to the United States via France. He was placed under surveillance there by the police, but could not be sent back to London to face trial since there was no extradition treaty at the time for his alleged crime. Physically he did not fit the description of Jack the Ripper given by any of the witnesses, and could not have murdered Mary Kelly on the 9th November (given that he had been arrested 2 days earlier).

PRINCE ALBERT CHRISTIAN EDWARD VICTOR

This highly publicised theory that formed the basis of several books, in particular the one by Stephen Knight, *Jack the Ripper: The Final Solution*, and also a feature film, *Murder by Decree*, has no place being treated as anything but fiction. Prince Victor, commonly known as Prince Eddy, was a grandson of Queen Victoria and had the formal title of the Duke of Clarence and Avondale as from 1891. He was known to be an enthusiastic deer-hunter (and hence had the required butchery skills to be Jack the Ripper), and also had an eye for the ladies.

It is conjectured that syphilis, contracted from one of his encounters, drove Prince Victor insane and that as a result he became Jack the Ripper, that this was known by other members of the Royal family, and that it was covered up, with Prince Victor eventually being put into an asylum (for which there is no evidence) on the Sandringham estate where he was to die in 1892.

However, at the time of the murders it can be proved beyond reasonable doubt that Prince Victor was as far away as Grosmont (Yorkshire), York, Abergeldie (Scotland) and Sandringham (Norfolk) unless one believes in a conspiracy theory.

A Singular Theory

'Theories! We were almost lost in theories; there were so many of them.'
Detective Inspector Abberline

Every 'Ripperologist' has their own theory as to the identity of Jack the Ripper. This author is no different and craves the reader's indulgence as he expounds a new theory predicated upon some questions which I believe were never answered satisfactorily at the time, and from where a logical train of thought leads via 11 premises not a named person *per se*, but to the direction the police investigation should have taken.

> 'Before we start to investigate, let us try to realize what we do know, so as to make the most of it, and to separate the essential from the accidental.'
> (Sherlock Holmes, *The Adventure of the Priory School*)

Why did the killings start in the first place, and why did they stop so suddenly? Although to the layperson serial killers may seem to be devoid of any logic, meaning, or motivation there is always a trigger. Condensing a complex subject into a few simple concepts, it can be said that serial killers are insecure individuals who are compelled to kill due to a morbid fear of rejection, often relating to a rejection by their mother in early childhood. They do not necessarily derive pleasure from their deeds, though they do commit them because they want to, and select victims based on availability, vulnerability, and desirability.

There are 7 basic motivations for serial killers:

- Anger (e.g. against a certain subgroup of people such as Jews).

- Criminal enterprise whereby the killer gains 'respect' (e.g. within a gang as well as monetary reward).

- Financial gain (e.g. multiple killings involving an insurance fraud).

- Ideology (e.g. this could relate to a gender, a religious or ethnic group of people).

- Power/thrill (where the killer feels empowered or exhilarated by their actions).

- Psychosis (where the killer has a severe mental illness which might include hallucinations, paranoia, or bizarre delusions).

- Sexual (where the motive is driven by sexual desire but may not need sexual contact).

All but 2 of these motivations might apply to Jack the Ripper. There seems to be no indication that either criminal enterprise or financial gain could have been a trigger for the Jack the Ripper murders.

> **Premise 1 – Jack the Ripper was somebody who died, or who was severely incapacitated, in late 1888 or early 1889.**

As to why the killings stopped, logically this can only be because (a) he/she died or could not continue (i.e. either accidental death, through ill health, suicide, death by natural causes, or murdered by somebody else), (b) he/she stopped of their own accord (i.e. they achieved what they wanted, or they had been cured), or (c) he/she went elsewhere (i.e. they went abroad, or were confined to an asylum/prison). In most cases the serial killer continues their work until they are caught (and often they want to be caught), and in the specific case of Jack the Ripper there is no convincing evidence to suggest either of the latter two propositions may be true, despite the conviction of Assistant Commissioner Robert Anderson that Jack the Ripper had been caught and been placed in an asylum without a trial (see page 96).

> **Premise 2 – Jack the Ripper worked alone and on foot. He did not have access to any private form of transport.**

Why were there not more sightings of Jack the Ripper? There were various descriptions of suspects given to the police, and one or more may have been correct, but in the main the descriptions seemed to contradict each other such that every foreigner, Jew, person who used a knife in their trade (e.g. 'Leather Apron') etc. was a suspect. Clearly, Jack the Ripper had a way of disappearing after each murder despite the increased police presence in the area. With the number of police officers and frequency of beat patrols (every 15 minutes or so) it seems incredible that nobody ever saw Jack the Ripper fleeing after the event, even though the police were often on the scene within minutes of an incident.

This has led to speculation that Jack the Ripper either had transport (such as a private carriage), or lived in the area. I believe neither to be correct. It is inconceivable that a horse drawn carriage (which immediately implies an accomplice) traversing the near empty streets of Whitechapel at such a time would not be heard, seen, or attract any attention, especially when the Whitechapel Division of the Metropolitan Police had well over 500 officers at their disposal in 1888.

A Singular Theory

> Premise 3 – Jack the Ripper did not live in Whitechapel, but knew of it, or travelled through it on a regular basis. His knowledge of the area was limited to the major thoroughfares, and for this reason when searching for victims he did not venture far from the main roads.

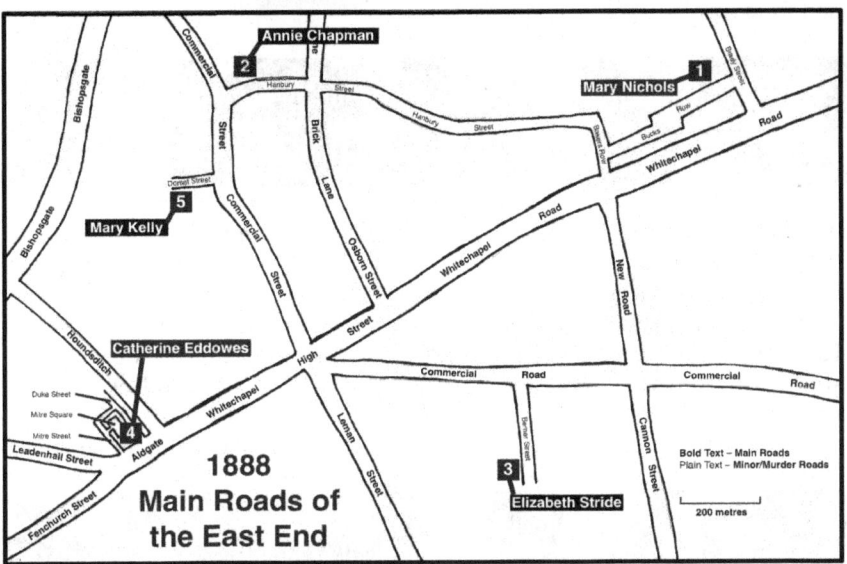

[Map illustrating the point that the canonical 5 attacks all took place adjacent to main roads running through the East End]

Most 'Ripperologists' are of the view that Jack the Ripper lived in Whitechapel, with at least one study looking at the murder sites and then by triangulation identifying the property in which he probably resided. The fact that is forgotten in this theory is that in such a small, densely populated area there was also a community, and that surely somebody, somewhere would have noticed a fellow lodger or neighbour of whom they had suspicions and would have reported that person to the police. It should also not be forgotten that the police carried out house-to-house searches, and also made extensive enquiries at the common lodging houses, all to no avail. There is a theory that if say Jack the Ripper was Jewish, as was the belief of Assistant Commissioner Robert Anderson (see page 96), then no matter how awful the deed he would not be given up by his fellow Jews to a Gentile.

If Jack the Ripper lived in Whitechapel it would be expected that he would know the area intimately. The killings of the canonical 5 victims all took place within

100 metres of the 3 main arteries running through the East End i.e. Whitechapel Road (and its extension into Whitechapel High Street and Aldgate High Street), Commercial Road, and Commercial Street. Hence, I conclude that he did not know Whitechapel that well since he did not venture far from the main roads and kept away from the filthy courts and alleyways. It can be further concluded that Jack the Ripper only knew of the area since he passed through it on his way to and from work.

> **Premise 4 – Jack the Ripper was a working man, probably within the City of London, and only had free time for his atrocities at weekends and around specific public holidays.**

The fact that Jack the Ripper was a working man can be inferred with reference to the dates of the murders, all of which took place at weekends or around public holidays – Polly Nichols was murdered on the Friday of a Bank Holiday weekend, Annie Chapman a Saturday, the night of the double event was a Sunday, and Mary Kelly was killed on the Friday of the Lord Mayor's Show (which for many workers in the City of London was also a public holiday). Hence Jack the Ripper not only lived outside of Whitechapel, but worked in the City of London and for this reason was limited in his options as to when he could commit his atrocities.

> **Premise 5 – Jack the Ripper escaped detection via the railway tracks and in so doing left no trail of blood.**

If Jack the Ripper did not live in the area how did he move about without leaving a trail of blood? Even if a body is cleanly cut into, and the Jack the Ripper victims were not, there would still be a substantial amount of blood which would inevitably find its way onto the murderer's clothes, and, in particular, their shoes? The blood would first soak into clothing, and, after a period of a few minutes, start to drip and leave a trail. Taking the death of Annie Chapman as an example (see page 25) the official report stated that not only was Annie's dress covered in blood, but so was the nearby fence and that there were 2 pools of blood next to the body. It is therefore inconceivable that Jack the Ripper did not get some blood on himself. To illustrate the point, in 1811 there was the horrific murder of the Timothy Marr family in their home along the Ratcliffe Highway – on exiting the house the murderer left a trail of blood that could be followed for half a mile.

The answer is obvious, but does raise some difficult questions to address – Jack the Ripper escaped undetected via the railways. Objectors would say immediately that there were no trains in the early hours of the morning, and they would be correct. However, Jack the Ripper did not need to board a train, only to gain access to the permanent way (the tracks), which at that time of day would be deserted (with the possible exception of railway gangs maintaining the tracks and the odd non-passenger train movement – both of which could be easily avoided).

There probably was a trail of blood to follow, but the police were looking in the wrong place. It may also have been that Jack the Ripper changed shoes/clothes after each murder (**Premise 10**). Members of the public did write in at the time and suggest that Jack the Ripper used the sewers as a means of escape, but this would not have been possible since (a) manhole covers are designed to be lifted by 2 persons, and (b) once in a sewer the manhole cover could not have been easily replaced – in fact, they are designed this way so that people cannot become trapped down a sewer.

> **Premise 6 – The canonical murders all took place within 400 metres of access points to railway lines. This provided an ideal method of escaping detection for Jack the Ripper.**

[Whitechapel station advertising its accessibility to all parts of London]

Taking **Premise 5** a step further, consider the very first murder, that of Polly Nichols (see page 15), which took place literally at the rear of Whitechapel station. The station had opened in 1876 for the East London Railway (Liverpool Street to Wapping going north to south) and was served by trains of 4 different railway companies (London, Brighton & South Coast Railway, Great Eastern Railway, London, Chatham & Dover Railway, and the South Eastern Railway). In 1884 the District Line extension from Mansion House terminated at Whitechapel (Mile End) station in a new building adjacent to the East London Railway. The latter withdrew its services between Whitechapel and Liverpool Street a year later. The District Line was not to be extended further eastward until 1902 when Stepney Green (part of the Whitechapel & Bow Railway) was opened. The station was not enclosed i.e. in a tunnel as were the next nearest Underground stations of St. Mary's and Aldgate East.

[Although called the Underground, due to its construction via the 'cut and cover' method and the use of steam locomotives, much of the railway ran in open shallow cuttings such as here near Farringdon (left), while there is only a modest drop from street level to platform level at Whitechapel station – the building in the picture (Trinity Hall) stands adjacent to where the body of Polly Nichols was found (right)]

Although the last passenger train would have been some time before midnight, the station would still have been accessible to staff, especially the permanent way gangs, so it would have been possible for Jack the Ripper to slip in and gain access to the tracks. Even if the front entrance was not yielding then it should be remembered that the line was built just below street level (via the cut and cover method of construction), and further that in order to let steam from the standing locomotives escape the station, which was a terminus at that time, Whitechapel was designed as an 'open' station.

As an alternative method of entry Jack the Ripper would only have had to negotiate a wall in Buck's Row, followed by a small drop down to platform level. If this failed there was also Spitalfields Coal Depot close by. Hence, using any of these means it would be possible for Jack the Ripper to gain access to the railway system and then walk along the tracks.

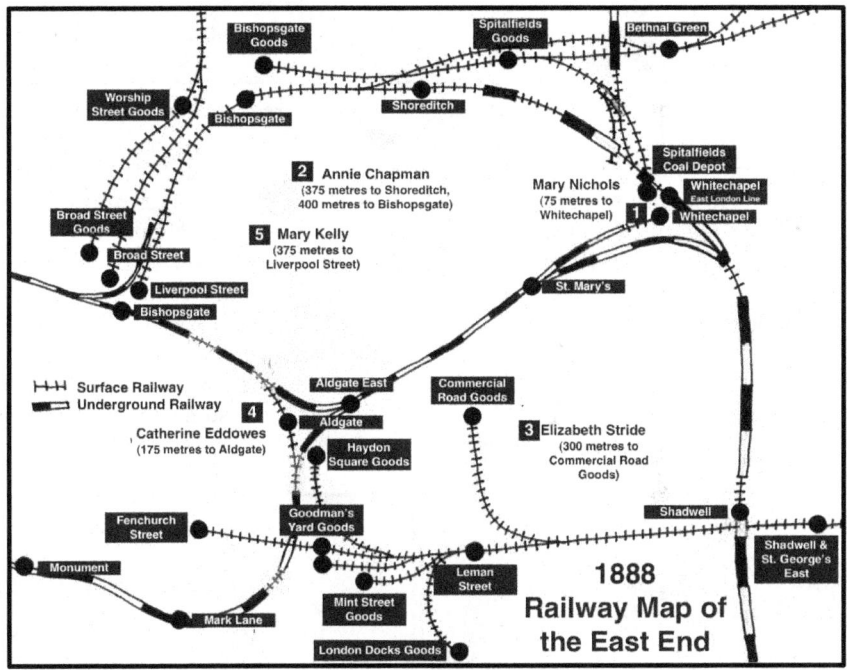

[Map showing that fortuitously, or perhaps by design, the canonical 5 victims were all murdered close to open sections of the railway network]

His options from Whitechapel station were either toward the City (northwest to Liverpool Street via the unused section of track of the East London Railway, or west to Aldgate East from where he could choose either the northern spur to join what is today the Circle Line toward Liverpool Street, or opt for the southern spur toward Mark Lane), or south to Wapping and potentially through the Thames Tunnel to south London.

In the Footsteps of Jack the Ripper

[Shoreditch station (left), and Liverpool Street station (right)]

Having (hopefully) convinced the reader that it was possible for Jack the Ripper to gain access to the railway tracks at Whitechapel the question remains whether the railways provided a means of escape for the other canonical murders? Annie Chapman's body (see page 21) was found in Hanbury Street with the closest railway stations being Liverpool Street (450 metres), Bishopsgate (400 metres) and Shoreditch (375 metres). All 3 stations were 'open' with Shoreditch being the smaller and quieter station as well as being the one accessible without having to traverse a major road. It should be pointed out that the railway line between all 3 stations ran over ground, in cuttings or on brick viaducts, so the tracks would be accessible along the whole of its length.

[Two views of the Commercial Road goods yard opened in 1887]

For Elizabeth Stride's murder (see page 29) just 300 metres away was the easily accessible goods yard at Commercial Road. However, this being the night of the double murder, Jack the Ripper may have elected not to use the railway in this case. If he did it would have been possible for him to enter the Commercial Road goods yard in east Goodman's Fields and emerge again at the Haydon Square depot in west Goodman's Fields.

[The remains of the Haydon Square spur in 2020]

If **Premise 11** is to be believed, Jack the Ripper would have needed to emerge here anyway since it was the closest he could get, without having to walk the streets, to the relative safety of the Underground at Aldgate (under 100 metres away). If he then found Catherine Eddowes (see page 34) in the vicinity of Aldgate High Street (having made her way back there upon her release from Bishopsgate police station), and subsequently murdered her in Mitre Square his closest railway access would still be Aldgate station only 150 metres away.

Again, having been a terminus at the time Aldgate was an 'open' station. This doesn't quite explain why Jack the Ripper would have gone past Aldgate toward Aldgate East station (which at that time was located around 200 metres to the west of its current location, albeit still completely enclosed) in order to dispose of the piece of Catherine Eddowes's apron and/or write the Goulston Street graffito (see page 38). It can be speculated that there was a policeman on his beat or other persons in the street blocking his access to Aldgate station, so Jack the Ripper fearing that he might be spotted (especially if covered in blood), took a risk and went past the station and into the nearest side alley to hide/wait for them to move on.

[The low wall in Blue Boar Alley (top left) gives easy access to the offices at Aldgate station (top right) and from there to the tracks below (bottom)]

It can then be conjectured that while waiting he came upon the idea of disposing of the apron/writing the graffito to misdirect the police (or maybe the piece of apron just fell from his clothing accidentally) before returning to the station when it was safe to do so. However, the most likely scenario, given that the apron had both blood and faeces on it, was that while waiting Jack the Ripper decided to clean himself up and wiped his hands and face upon the apron before disposing of it, probably without any thought as to the implications of discarding it adjacent to the graffito (which he almost certainly did not write).

[In 2020 Aldgate remains an 'open' station, hemmed in between 2 office blocks which dominate the area]

The death of Mary Kelly (see page 44) does present a problem as this killing was further than most from a station, and had no safe route – Aldgate (400 metres) and Liverpool Street (375 metres to the main entrance). However, Jack the Ripper had no control over this since when he met Mary in the vicinity of Flower and Dean Street or Thrawl Street (both of which are closer to Aldgate station) he would not have known that she would take him back to her lodgings in Miller's Court. As this murder took place indoors it was not so hazardous for Jack the Ripper who would have had time to change his clothes and clean himself up before leaving for a station. He may have deemed it better to take advantage of the opportunity to perform a 'proper job' indoors, albeit further from an exit route.

Premise 7 – Jack the Ripper had an intimate knowledge of the railways and may be, or had been at some time, a railway worker.

[Could Jack the Ripper have been a railway worker
such as the plate layers shown here?]

It has already been noted under **Premise 3** that Jack the Ripper did not stray far from the main thoroughfares in the East End, which led to the conclusion that he had no great knowledge of the area. Combining this with **Premise 6** implies that Jack the Ripper probably had an in-depth knowledge of the railways i.e. both the lines and the nature of the stations ('open' or 'closed'), as well as how to gain access to them. Hence the inevitable conclusion is that he was, or had been, a railway worker.

Premise 8 – If Jack the Ripper was a railwayman his killing spree might have been brought to an end by a railway accident (fatal or otherwise).

If Jack the Ripper was a railway worker it may provide an explanation of why the murders stopped so suddenly, since working on the lines was a hazardous job with many deaths and injuries each year. Most accidents were caused by human error, and this is not surprising. Looking at the railway records for 1883 it shows that enginemen and firemen would work between 10 hours and 18 hours a day, occasionally on a Sunday, and only receive 2 or 3 days of holiday a year. Other ranks faired little better with no railway employee working less than 10 hours a day.

Turning to the official accident reports there were at total of 76 incidents in 1888. On the 1st December a train was derailed due to excessive speed at Liverpool Street station, while on the 31st December 19 people were injured at Norwood Junction (South London) in fog, and on the same day 51 were injured due to insufficient brakes at Loughborough Junction (South London) when a train overran a red signal. The next London incident was on the 16th January 1889 when there was a buffer stop collision at Moorgate Street resulting in 10 persons being injured, followed on the 28th January by a broken rail incident at Stoke Newington (North London) when 32 people were injured. Even more dangerous than being a passenger on a train, was to be a permanent way worker with accidents and fatalities going largely unrecorded. Hence, it is possible that the activities of Jack the Ripper were curtailed by one of the frequent railway accidents of the time.

If, as some maintain, the last Jack the Ripper killings were those on the night of the double event on the 30th September 1888 then a specific railway incident presents itself, for on the 26th October that year at Bow Road a signalling error caused 8 injuries. In that instance the 7.08 p.m. goods train from Poplar to Hampstead, while being held at a signal at Bow Road, was run into at the rear by the 7.25 p.m. passenger train from Fenchurch Street to North Woolwich.

Premise 9 – Jack the Ripper only started his killings in 1888 since it was only then that the railways provided easy, and cheap, access from where he lived (Laindon or the Gospel Oak area) to the East End.

The railways might also give an explanation, at least a partial one, concerning why the killings started when they did. **Premise 3** made it clear that Jack the Ripper most likely worked in the City of London, but lived outside to the East so he would commute through Whitechapel, even if he did not know it intimately. Laindon railway station, on the direct route (not the loop via Tilbury) between Barking and Pitsea was opened on the 1st June 1888. Then, as today, it was a commuter station and would have been used by workmen taking the 22 miles trip to Fenchurch Street (passing through the East End) for which special low-priced tickets at under a farthing per mile of travel were available. Southend-on-Sea at the other end of the line was a popular destination for day trippers from the East End with records showing that around 25,000 people made the journey (via Tilbury) on the Bank Holiday weekend of 1887, again at a special low fare. Records also show that in 1892 there were between 2,000 and 3,000 workmen buying workmen tickets at 3d. return for the 7 mile journey from Barking to

Fenchurch Street every day. It could be that Jack the Ripper had no access to London before 1888, and only started his killing spree because as from June 1888 he had easy, and cheap, access to Whitechapel. At that time the last weekday trains into Fenchurch Street arrived just before midnight (around 10.30 p.m. on a Sunday), and the earliest departure was just before 6.00 a.m. (9.00 a.m. on a Sunday).

However, this theory has a major flaw to overcome, since the summer of 1888 had seen so much rain that waters had spread over the flat fields of Essex causing an embankment to collapse between Laindon and West Horndon with the consequence that through railway traffic was suspended from mid-August until the winter. Jack the Ripper would have been forced to travel to London via Pitsea and the Tilbury loop – a much longer journey, though still possible.

Perhaps a better station candidate, and much closer to Whitechapel, would be the Tottenham & Hampstead Junction Railway to Gospel Oak which operated into Broad Street (and Moorgate Street with a change of train). Gospel Oak station was opened on the 4th June 1888. Whether he used Fenchurch Street, Broad Street, or Moorgate Street stations, Jack the Ripper could easily reach Whitechapel on foot having arrived via the last train of the day.

> **Premise 10 – Jack the Ripper wore workman's clothes and possibly carried a tool bag just like thousands of others in the area, and for that reason drew no attention to himself. Maybe he disguised himself as a railway worker.**

There have been many descriptions of how Jack the Ripper was dressed, but unfortunately the various reports tend to contradict each other. The fact that Jack the Ripper was able to move about freely without attracting attention prior to each murder indicates that he did not look out of place in the East End. Certainly, he was not as he is shown in popular culture, a man in a cloak and top hat ready for the opera (see page 49). It is far more likely that he dressed as a workman (see page 39). It can also be conjectured that he carried a workman's bag, since he surely needed some receptacle in which to place the body parts he took? The knife used by Jack the Ripper was estimated to have a blade only 6 inches long, and so this could have been concealed about his person prior to an attack, but afterwards, being covered in blood, it would have been more convenient to place it in a bag. I propose that he may have kept a spare set of outer garments, and even shoes, in the bag in order to avoid leaving a trail of blood from the scene of crime (**Premise 5**). These he would have time and privacy to change into once he reached the relative safety of the railway tracks. The type of workman on the streets at that time of night would include those employed to maintain the permanent way on the railways as well as those working on the roads.

[Could Jack the Ripper have avoided suspicion by dressing as a labourer with a tool bag such as these men laying new pipes – a job frequently done at night?]

Summary

In summary thus far, the profile of the suspect being sought is that of a loner from outside the Whitechapel area who worked in the City of London, possibly with a railway connection, who lived within commuting distance of central London (possibly Laindon or Gospel Oak areas) who was to die, or be incapacitated, (possibly in a railway accident) in late 1888 or early 1889. In any event they dressed in workman's clothes, and with their knowledge of the railways were able to use open stations/sections of track to escape the scene of crime undetected.

This still leaves 2 major questions unanswered:

- Did Jack the Ripper have any anatomical knowledge, and if so how did he acquire it?
- On the night of the double event did Jack the Ripper wander aimlessly after the first killing, or was he heading in a specific direction?

> **Premise 11** – Jack the Ripper worked at Smithfield Market, which he could easily access via the Underground railway network undetected. Here he would not look out of place with blood-stained clothes, and in addition he would also be familiar with using a knife, and possess a rudimentary knowledge of animal anatomy.

Addressing the second question first, I believe that Jack the Ripper acted with definite purpose and was heading toward the City of London for a very good reason – having done his 'work' for the evening (albeit interrupted) he was going to his other place of work. It would provide shelter and somewhere to clean himself up before going home once passenger train services commenced later in the day. If, as suspected, following the murder of Elizabeth Stride he went from the Commercial Road goods depot along the track to the Haydon Square goods yard, then killed Catherine Eddowes after which he re-entered the railway system at Aldgate station (via a diversion to Goulston Street) Jack the Ripper had two choices of route. He could elect to go north via Liverpool Street, or south via Mark Lane.

Looking at the Underground stations in both directions, two locations at $4/5^{th}$ and $1 1/3^{rd}$ rail miles respectively, rather obviously present themselves. The first, and the shorter of the 2 options, leads to Billingsgate Fish Market where suspect Joseph Barnett (see page 93) had worked. However, this location presents a problem since the closest station would have been Mark Lane which was a fully 'closed' station so Jack the Ripper would have had a major difficulty in exiting. Even if he did, there was then a walk of nearly half a mile through the streets of the City to the market.

[Smithfield Market in Dickensian times (left) prior to the opening of the London Central Meat Market in 1868 (right)]

The second location, although further away, has several advantages. It had been described in 1843 by Thomas Maslen thus, 'of all the horrid abominations with which London has been cursed, there is not one that can come up to that disgusting place, West Smithfield Market, for cruelty, filth, effluvia, pestilence, impiety, horrid language, danger, disgusting and shuddering sights, and every obnoxious item that can be imagined; and this abomination is suffered to continue year after year, from generation to generation, in the very heart of the most Christian and most polished city in the world'.

[A recent photograph showing the various tunnels in the Smithfield area – to the left are the Circle and Metropolitan Underground tracks serving Barbican station, while those to the right (and covered) were those running underneath, and dedicated to, Smithfield Market (seen behind)]

Entry to London's main meat market would have been simplicity itself for Jack the Ripper since there were a series of sidings from the main line that ran beneath Smithfield Park which were used for the transfer of animal carcasses to its cold store with direct access to the meat market via lifts. Hence Jack the Ripper could have reached his workplace without ever having to be seen on the streets of London. Furthermore, from here he could have walked to either Moorgate Street or Broad Street stations to catch a train back to his home in the Gospel Oak area, or even Fenchurch Street for Laindon (**Premise 9**).

[The interior and exterior of the main hall at
Smithfield Market in Victorian time]

Smithfield, which covered 10 acres, opened at around 2 a.m. each trading day, but would not have been in operation at weekends or on Bank Holidays (including the day of the Lord Mayor's Show since it was a Corporation of the City of London building). According to Charles Dickens in *Oliver Twist*, 'the ground was covered, nearly ankle-deep, with filth and mire; a thick steam perpetually rising from the reeking bodies of the cattle ... the unwashed, unshaven, squalid and dirty figures constantly running to and fro, and bursting in and out of the throng, rendered it a stunning and bewildering scene, which quite confounded the senses'. *Oliver Twist* was published in 1837 when live cattle were taken to the market, a practice that stopped in 1855.

By the time of Jack the Ripper things had improved with the opening of the London Central Meat Market in 1868, but even so somebody with blood on them would not have looked out of place here in 1888. Incidentally, the Annexe Market building, used as a fish market, only came into operation in 1888, so again it may be that Jack the Ripper only came to London as a result of the opening of this part of the market. Indeed, it all fits together nicely and answers the first question. If Jack the Ripper were a market porter (such as suspect Joseph Barnett had been – see page 93), or worked for one of the traders in the market, he would doubtless know how to use a knife, and if in the meat market would also have a knowledge of animal anatomy.

Conclusion

In conclusion, Jack the Ripper was a loner from outside the Whitechapel area, who worked at Smithfield Market in the City of London, and lived within commuting distance of the City of London (possibly Laindon, but more likely the Gospel Oak area). He knew how to use a knife, and possessed a basic knowledge of animal anatomy. He also had an excellent knowledge of the railways, and may have been a railwayman prior to working at the market. He died, or was incapacitated, (possibly in a railway accident) in late 1888 or early 1889. He dressed in workman's clothes to avoid raising suspicion, and with his knowledge of the railways was able to use open stations/sections of track to escape the scene of crime undetected and without leaving a blood trail.

N.B. This, like all the other 'Ripperologist' theories, is pure speculation and cannot be proved ... or disproved. In the words of Sherlock Holmes in *A Study in Scarlet* ...

'It is a capital mistake to theorize before you have all the evidence.
It biases the judgment.'

A FINAL THOUGHT

Irrespective of whether you, as the reader, believe that any/all of the murderers in this book were committed by the infamous Jack the Ripper, or that the perpetrator was caught/identified either at the time, or more recently, you are probably comforted by the thought that at least nothing else like that has, or could possibly, happen again in London – well think again, and consider the following ...

Dr. Thomas Neill Cream (1850-1892) – Serial killer known as the Lambeth Poisoner operating between 1881 and 1891. He was convicted of 5 murders and suspected of at least 5 more. He was a sadist motivated by money (and also a candidate for being Jack the Ripper – see page 94). His poison of choice was strychnine.

John Haigh (1909-1949) – Serial killer of 6 people (possibly 9) between 1944 and 1949 who were either battered to death or shot then dissolved in a drum of sulphuric acid. Motivation was so he could forge their signatures on documents and obtain their property and other possessions of value.

John Christie (1899-1953) – Serial killer of at least 8 persons, including his wife and a 13-month old baby girl, between 1943 and 1953. Victims were lured to his kitchen where they were rendered unconscious with domestic gas prior to strangulation. Some were raped while unconscious. Eight of the bodies were found at his residence of 10 Rillington Place, W11.

Graham Young (1947-1990) – Obsessed with chemistry he first poisoned 3 members of his family (his step-mother dying from a dose of antimony administered in a cup of tea) in Neasden in 1962. Hence, he became known as 'The Teacup Poisoner'. He was caught and served time in prison, but on release worked at Hadland Laboratories where he poisoned 70 of his colleagues (2 of which died). In 1972 he was again back in prison, and this time he died there in 1990.

Jack the Stripper (unknown) – Serial killer of at least 6 women prostitutes, all found naked near the river in West London between 1964 and 1965. The case was also known as the Hammersmith Nude Murders. Most of the women had been strangled. Despite a large police investigation and many suspects, including police officers, nobody was ever convicted of the killings. The most likely suspect was a security guard named Mungo Ireland who committed suicide leaving a note to say he could not bear the strain any longer. More recent evidence, though suggests that he may not have been the murderer.

Dennis Nilsen (1945-2018) – Serial killer and necrophile operating out of 23 Cranley Gardens, N10 and 195 Melrose Avenue, NW2. Responsible for 'fifteen or sixteen bodies, since 1978. It's a relief to get it off my mind'. The murders, which included boys as well as men, took place between 1978 and 1983 and were sexually motivated. His *modus operandi* was to pick up his victim (often a homeless person) in a pub, take them home, ply them with food and alcohol, strangle them until they were unconscious, drown them in his bath, dismembering them, and burn their body parts in the garden or flush them away down the toilet.

Michele de Marco Lupo (1953-1995) – Dubbed 'The Wolfman', Lupo claimed to have had 4,000 lovers and was responsible for the murder of at least 4 gay men in the 1980s. He worked for Yves Saint Laurent in Brompton Road, Kensington. In 1987 he was sentenced to 4 terms of life imprisonment, and subsequently died in prison from an AIDS related illness in 1995. His medical condition led him to have a loathing of fellow homosexuals which led him developing a 'callous rationale' and an 'urge to kill'.

Kenneth Erskine (1963-) – Better known as the 'Stockwell Strangler', Erskine murdered at least 7 pensioners in South London, many of whom had been strangled, beaten and sodomised. He operated between April and July 1986. He was imprisoned in 1988 with a recommended minimum term of 40 years, but has since been diagnosed with chronic schizophrenia and antisocial personality disorder and transferred to Broadmoor Hospital where he should remain for the rest of his life.

Levi Bellfield (1968-) – The 'Bus Stop Stalker' murdered Milly Dowler and at least 2 others, and was suspected of a string of abductions, rapes, and murders across West London in the late 1990s and early 2000s. He ran a wheel-clamping business in West London, and would cruise the streets in his car hoping to pick up girls at bus stops by offering them a lift home. Has been in prison since 2011 with a recommendation that he should never be released.

Anthony Hardy (1951-) – Convicted of 3 murders in 2003, and sentenced to 3 life sentences. Known as the 'Camden Ripper' he was responsible for the deaths of 2 women who were found outside his flat stuffed into bin-bags, and another battered woman found in his bed. It is also possible that he was the culprit in the deaths 2 prostitutes who were found dismembered and dumped in the Thames, and up to 5 or 6 other murders which bore marked resemblances to the ones for which he was convicted.

On the basis that every decade since Jack the Ripper has seen at least one new serial killer on the streets of the Capital, just like London buses, another must be due very soon!

JACK THE RIPPER WALKS

Both tours use the What3Words (3 words in bold with round brackets) application to identify locations as accurately as possible, and include page references (bold numbers with round brackets) and photographic references (bold numbers with square brackets). Although much safer than in 1888, it should be noted that the tours are set in non-tourist areas of London with a higher than average crime rate – please take this into consideration when planning your visit.

THE CANONICAL FIVE WALK

Duration: 2-3 hours
Start: Whitechapel station   **Finish:** Liverpool Street station

As its name suggests, this walk covers locations of the murders of Mary Nichols, Annie Chapman, Elizabeth Stride, Catherine Eddowes, and Mary Kelly and other associated places of interest along the way. Unlike many other tours it covers the locations in a chronological order. It is done entirely on foot and covers several miles of flat terrain.

🐾 1 🐾
MARY NICHOLS - DURWARD STREET
⇐ 15 minutes ⇒

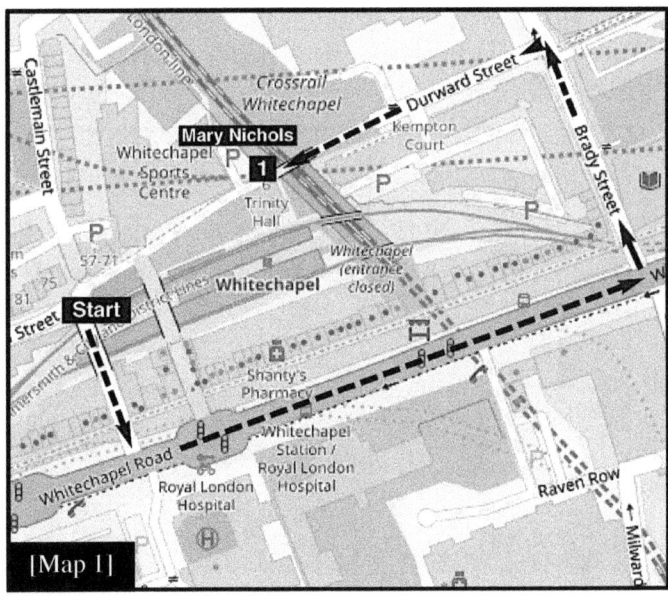

[Map 1]

123

From the Whitechapel station entrance in Court Street (**ahead.smile.farm**) [Map 1] turn right and proceed over the railway line and down the steps to Whitechapel Road (**20**). Immediately in front of you on the opposite side of the road is the Victorian façade of the Royal London Hospital where Emma Smith was taken for examination (**64**). Turn left and walk along Whitechapel Road. You will soon pass the King Edward VII Memorial (**café.safe.person**) [**1**].

This drinking fountain is a reminder that the population of the area was mainly Jewish, for it was erected 'from subscriptions raised by Jewish inhabitants of the East End' and unveiled in 1912 by Charles Rothschild. The design includes bronze figures of the Angel of Peace [**2**], and the Angel of Justice with 2 cherubs – one has a needle and thread indicating the importance of the clothing industry to the area, and the other is reading a book signifying the importance of education [**3**]. On the opposite side is the Angel of Liberty also with 2 cherubs – one holds a ship to indicate that many locals were recently immigrants, while the second has a car illustrating progress away from the horse and cart [**4**].

A little further along you will come to the original entrance to Whitechapel Station (**105**), adjacent to which is the Working Lads' Institute (**remedy.fines.simple**) (**[5]** and **[6]**). This is where the inquest into the murder of Mary Nichols was held. When opened in 1885 its purpose was to keep young lads out of trouble and to provide academic classes. There was a fully equipped gym, a library, a large swimming pool, and even limited accommodation.

Carry on along Whitechapel Road to the next intersection (Brady Street). Turn left into Brady Street, and then (opposite Sainsbury's) turn left again into Durward Street (**15**). Next to the Durward Street exit to Whitechapel station (**jolly.orange.monks**) is where Mary Nichols' body was discovered (**15-16**) [7].

☙ 2 ❧
ANNIE CHAPMAN - HANBURY STREET
⇐20 minutes ⇒

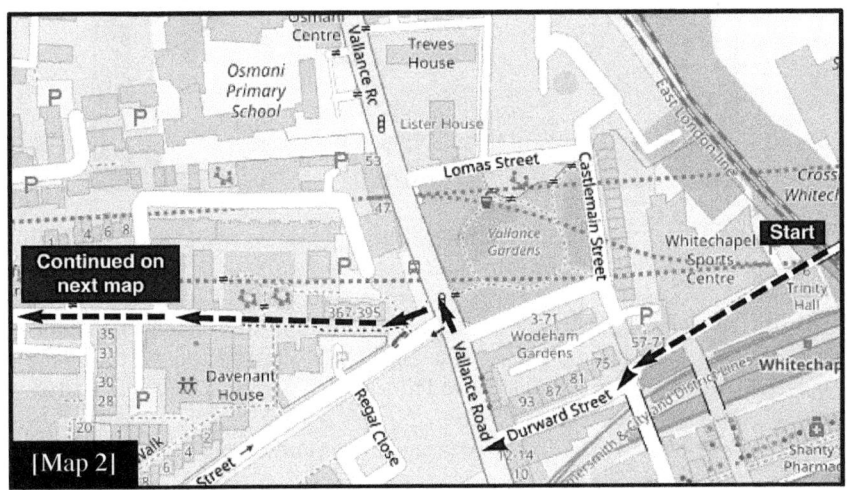

Carry on down Durward Street [**Map 2**] passing the former Buck's Row Board School building which is now a block of residential flats called Trinity Hall (**filled.noise.zest**) [**8**].

At the end of Durward Street turn right into Vallance Road. The next turning on the left is Old Montague Street and here you will also see the start of Hanbury Street (**28**) – actually a bicycle path which goes off to the right between two large blocks of flats. It is at this end of Hanbury Street that Police Constable Jonas Mizen, while on his beat, was told about Mary Nichols by the 2 workmen, Charles Cross and Robert Paul (**15**).

Walk along here and into Hanbury Street proper passing the Chicksand Estate (Hanbury Street) flats. You will note that the development was built in 1974 by the Greater London Council [**9**].

On the left you will pass the Brady Girls Club and Settlement, and the Brady Boys Club (**adopt.play.tilt**) [**10**]. The latter was the first Jewish boys' club in the country being founded in 1896 by, among others, Lady Charlotte Rothschild. Initially the club was housed in a disused vicarage in Whitechapel with the purpose of giving recreational and educational opportunities, and a chance to go on holiday to a summer camp. It moved to Hanbury Street in 1938 and shared the building with the Brady Girls Club which was started here in 1936. Today the building is the home to the Brady Arts and Community Centre [**11**].

A little further along Hanbury Street on the right is the old Deal Street school (**pots.evenly.purple**), which was built in 1895 **[12]** by the London School Board. When opened in 1896 it was designed for 1,200 pupils, cost £16,945 to build and, because of the shortage of space, had a playground constructed on the roof **[13]**. Today it is the Montefiore Centre, an establishment for education and training. The next block of flats on the right-hand-side of the road exhibits a piece of civic pride in the form of the sign and crest on the side of Hanbury House**[14]**.

Hanbury Street now bears to the right at the junction with Greatorex Street [**Map 3**]. The next left turn is Spelman Street where on the corner in 1888 stood The Alma public house **[15]**. Annie Chapman was known to be a regular at this notorious establishment, and just prior to her murder was seen close by to here in the company of a man who was almost certainly Jack the Ripper (**24**).

Jack the Ripper Walks

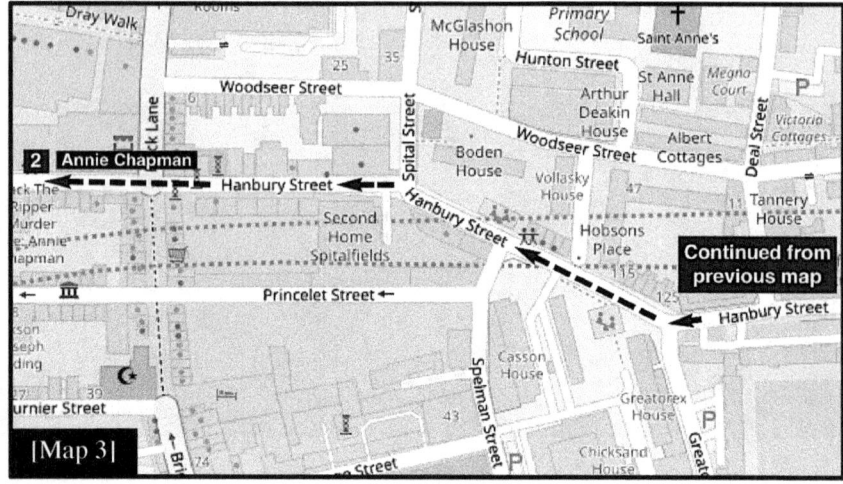

[Map 3]

As the road bends to the left you enter a section of Hanbury Street which is much more atmospheric and Victorian in appearance, but not before you pass an orange 1970s looking building (**trend.same.pots**) **[16]**. This is Second Home, a coworking space for small businesses (the coffee shop of which is open to the public). Note from the sign that you have passed out of Whitechapel and are now firmly in the Spitalfields area of east London.

The next intersection is Brick Lane (**64**). As you cross over the road look to your right and you will see a reminder of the old Truman Brewery (**24**). It was on the right-hand-side just past the intersection (**shell.ahead.doing**) that the body of Annie Chapman was discovered at the back of No. 29 Hanbury Street (**21-24**), opposite Nos. 30-32 in the modern street numbering **[17]**.

128

👣 3 👣
ELIZABETH STRIDE - HENRIQUES STREET
⇐ 45 minutes ⇒

As you continue down Hanbury Street [**Map 4**] you will pass Hanbury Hall (**teeth.past.pushed**) [**18**]. Notice the tiles embedded in the wall which are a reminder of the former Huguenot influence in the area [**19**]. It was built in 1719 as a small French Huguenot chapel, but over the years it became La Patente Church (1740), a German Lutheran Church (1787), and a United Free Methodists Church prior to becoming part of the Anglican Christ Church in 1887. Charles

Dickens was no stranger to the building, using it for public readings of his works, and in 1888 it was here that the 'match girls' (**60**) held their strike meetings as they began their protest for better working conditions at the nearby Bryant and May factory in Bow.

Continue on, and just past Wilkes Street on the left-hand-side is No. 12 Hanbury Street (**pushed.showed.longer**) which, as the blue plaque indicates, was where Bud Flanagan, the popular music hall and vaudeville entertainer, was born [**20**]. He was best known as being part of the 'Crazy Gang', and as half the double act Flanagan and (Chesney) Allen in the 1930s to 1950s.

At the end of Hanbury Street is Commercial Street. Here you can make a short optional detour to the right. If you do this the next turning on the left will be Folgate Street on the corner of which is an imposing triangular-shaped building (**wonderfully.gazed.cowboy**) [**21**]. This is the very first Model Dwellings establishment opened by the Peabody Donation Fund in 1864 (**42**). Continue up to the next turning on the left (Fleur de Lis Street) and a similar styled building with Portland stone facing to the ground floor and set on a triangular piece of land can be seen (**loss.minute.pushed**) [**22**]. This was Commercial Street police station and dates from 1874 (with the upper storey not being added until 1906). Note the inscription '*dieu et mon droit*' above what was the main entrance [**23**]. Along with Leman Street and Bishopsgate it was one of the 3 key police stations during the Jack the Ripper investigations. Its most famous occupant was Detective Inspector Frederick Abberline.

Retrace your steps passing Hanbury Street which will now be on your left. When you reach No. 92 Commercial Street on the left-hand-side of the road, look up and you will see a brown plaque to mark where Nicholas Culpeper, the physician, herbalist, astrologer, and writer, lived and worked in the 17th century (**skills.pulled.drape**) [**24**].

On the opposite side of the road are entrances to Spitalfields Market [**25**] which has been trading since 1638. Originally for the sale of 'flesh, fowl and roots', today it is popular for fashion, arts and crafts, and general goods. There are several food outlets as well as public toilets. You may like to explore the market further, or continue to the Ten Bells public house [**26**] located on the corner of Fournier Street (**tunes.ridge.coins**). Either way please note that you will return here towards the end of the tour for the murder site of Mary Kelly (victim No. 5) is literally just around the corner.

The Ten Bells is where Mary Kelly was seen drinking with Elizabeth Foster on the night of her murder (**45**), but this popular drinking hole would have been known by all the victims of Jack the Ripper. It was established in 1755 (as the Eight Bells) adjacent to where it now stands, and moved to its current location in 1851 when Commercial Street was cut. The name refers to the peel of bells at Christ Church opposite which until 1788 had just 8 bells, then 10 bells, and finally an even dozen. However, in 1836 there was a fire at the church which reduced that number by 4. Hence, the public house should more accurately revert to its original name. The interior is pure Victorian with some original blue and white floral pattern tiling, and a mural entitled *Spitalfields in ye Olden Time – visiting a Weaver's Shop* thus commemorating the weaving heritage of the area. This premises has always been a magnet for Jack the Ripper enthusiasts, and it even featured in a scene of the 1999 film *From Hell* in which Detective Inspector Frederick Abberline (played by Johnny Depp) has a drink with Mary Kelly.

The whole area of Spitalfields is dominated by Nicholas Hawksmoor's Christ Church (**dizzy.wins.reason**) [**27**] built between 1714 and 1729 to show an Anglican presence in a predominantly Huguenot part of London. In time the Huguenots too would come to worship here as is evident by the number of gravestones with French names in the graveyard. The nave [**28**] was described as being a very plain rectangular box albeit with Composite order columns, a richly decorated flat ceiling, and clerestory to allow natural lighting. Looking at this magnificent building in 2020 it is hard to believe that in 1960 the church was nearly derelict and in urgent need of restoration. The crypt became a rehabilitation centre for homeless alcoholic men until 2000. Today it has disabled access which leads to a café which is open to the public and highly recommended.

From the Ten Bells in Commercial Street turn left into Fournier Street and proceed along its full length to Brick Lane. The street, with its Georgian townhouses, has changed little since the 1720s when it became a fashionable road for Huguenots involved with the silk trade **[29]**. Originally called Church Street, it was renamed after one such Huguenot, George Fournier, while currently one of its most celebrated residents is another George, George Passmore who lives at No. 12 with fellow artist Gilbert Proesch. You might like to note that the numbering of at least one property is very Harry Potteresque (**grow.silks.target**)**[30]**.

Turn right into Brick Lane (**64**) and almost immediately you will see the blue plaque at No. 55 commemorating the family home of Haroon Shamsher, founder of Joi, an alternative dub/dance music DJ team he set up with his brother Farook (**kinds.mini.boat**) **[31]**. A little further along, and also on the right-hand-side, is Christ Church School which dates from 1873 (**solve.slips.arch**) **[32]**.

The next street down on the right-hand-side is Fashion Street (**clean.tanks.surely**), and it is here that many seeking out the locations of Jack the Ripper can become confused, for the street layouts have changed almost beyond recognition since 1888, though the street names have been retained. Between here and Wentworth Street (which is the next street down on the right) used to be Flower and Dean Street, and Thrawl Street running parallel to each other, while running across these 2 roads and intersecting with Wentworth Street was George Street (where Mary Kelly (**45**), and Emma Smith (**62**) may both have lived for a while). However, there is an anomaly here since maps dating from 1860 and 1900 show George Street ending at Flower and Dean Street, whereas intermediate maps from 1890 show it running through to Fashion Street. It should also be noted that by 1900 George Street had become Lolesworth Street. Another problem arises as there were no fewer than 3 George Streets in the area: to the east of Brick Lane and running parallel to the one that became Lolesworth Street was the 2nd George Street, but this road was renamed Casson Street in 1883, while the final George Street was closer to Commercial Road and the St. George Brewery (and is, in fact, the one in which Mary Kelly lodged).

Fashion Street itself was laid out in the middle of the 17th century and was originally called Fossan Street after brothers Thomas and Lewis who owned large portions of land here. It later became corrupted to Fashion Street so its name has nothing to do with the clothing industry as many assume. It was an address in

Jack the Ripper Walks

Fashion Street that Catherine Eddowes falsely gave as her abode to the police when released from Bishopsgate police station on the night of her murder (**35**). The arcade on the south side of the street [**33**] dates from 1905 and was the idea of Abraham Davis who intended to build 2 such covered structures with cross-passages that would contain 250 small shops. In the end only 63 were finished and by 1909 he had gone bankrupt.

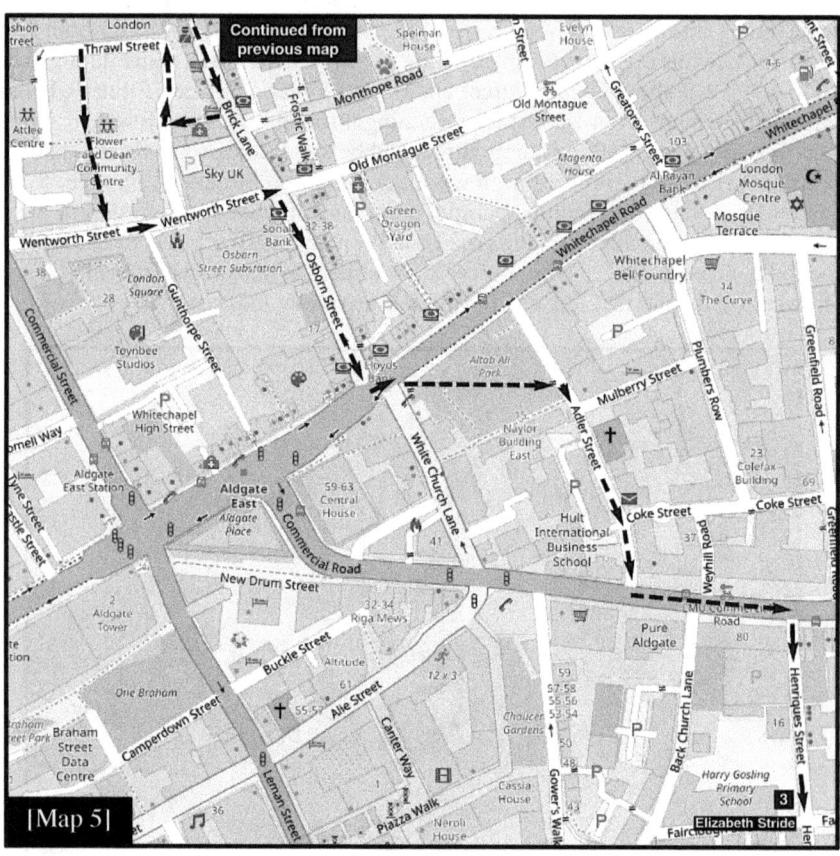

[Map 5]

Proceed down Brick Lane [**Map 5**]. The next turning on your left is Chicksand Street (named after a village in Bedfordshire). It was opposite here (by No. 25 Brick Lane (**chart.sock.melon**)) that Flower and Dean Street connected with Commercial Street. Today behind these modern flats is Thrawl Street. This is because when the new estate was built Thrawl Street was designated to run around the perimeter forming the shape of an upside-down toilet 'U' bend. Carry on down Brick Lane a little further until just before the iron arch over the street.

Here on the right-hand-side you will find an Indian restaurant (**spoken.planet.olive**) [**34**]. If you look up you will see the original name of this establishment was The Frying Pan, the public house where Mary Nichols was seen just prior to her murder (**18**). At the side of the building is an alley which you should go down [**35**]. This was the original Thrawl Street which connected with Commercial Street (which can be seen in the distance). It was in this street that Mary Nichols resided (**18**), and from where, shortly before her demise, she was ejected for not having sufficient funds to pay for her night's accommodation. It is also the street in which Mary Kelly resided for a short time (**45**), and in which direction she was heading when approached by Jack the Ripper (**47**). Frances

Coles also lodged in Thrawl Street (**84**), and just a few hours before her murder had asked her landlady if she could return there if she paid her rent arrears. Later that same evening her man friend, James Sadler, was mugged here (**85**).

At the end of the alley turn right (which is also Thrawl Street) and just follow the road around the corner (still Thrawl Street) [**36**]. As you turn the corner you are now approximately where Flower and Dean Street was located. Elizabeth Stride resided in a common lodging house at No. 32 Flower and Dean Street (**29**), while Catherine Eddowes was further up the road at No. 55 (**34**). Immediately before her encounter with Jack the Ripper in Thrawl Street, Mary Kelly was spotted by George Hutchinson in Flower and Dean Street (**47**). Another person spotted in this road on the night of their death was Alice McKenzie (**77**).

Half way along this section of road you will see Flower and Dean Walk on your left [**37**]. Go into Flower and Dean Walk (which would have been George Street, and latterly Lolesworth Street) and walk to the far end which is the intersection with Wentworth Street.

You will have just passed under a brick arch (**plus.sports.level**) which was the former entrance to the Rothschild Buildings in Flower and Dean Street [**38**]. It was relocated here as a reminder of those model dwellings which were erected by the Four Per Cent Industrial Dwelling Company Ltd. in 1886 (**42**). There is another reminder of the past if you look up and down Wentworth Street [**39**] and compare it to the picture on page 9 of how the road appeared to Gustave Doré in 1869.

Turn left along Wentworth Street until it comes to the intersection with Brick Lane where you will turn right into Osborn Street. At the end is Whitechapel High Street and on the corner you will note Jack the Chipper take away (**local.settle.skinny**) [**40**]. The last sighting of Mary Nichols was at the intersection with the main road (**erase.data.leaned**). It was here that she talked with fellow prostitute Emily Holland (**19**).

Almost opposite you will see an open space. It is, in fact, Altab Ali Park (formerly St. Mary's Park) which occupies the site of the 14th century white church of St. Mary Matfelon from which the name Whitechapel is derived (**piles.piano.regime**). The church was destroyed in World War II so that all that remains is the floor plan and a few scattered graves [**41**]. Cross the road, and walk diagonally across the park, and turn right into Adler Street. At the end of Adler Street turn left into Commercial Road, and then take the second right into Henriques Street (formerly Berner Street).

As you pass down the street you will see the Harry Gosling Primary School on your right-hand-side. Just past the bottom school gate (**enter.quest.tinsel**) would have been the entrance to Dutfield's Yard where the body of Elizabeth Stride was discovered (**29**). On the opposite side of the street is Bernhard Baron House, another reminder that the area was predominantly Jewish [**42**]. Note the plaque in memory of those members of the West London and Liberal Jewish Synagogue who gave their lives during World War I.

☙ 4 ☙
CATHERINE EDDOWES - MITRE SQUARE
⇐25 minutes ⇒

From Henriques Street [**Map 6**] turn right into Fairclough Street keeping the school on your left. You may like to note the mosaic celebrating 100 years of the school dating from 2010 (**plays.flood.death**) [**43**]. At the end of the street turn left into Back Church Lane. Here you will note several fine Victorian former warehouses such as the one belonging to Charles Kinloch & Co. Limited (**invest.ahead.usage**) [**44**]. The warehouses were located here because they backed onto the Commercial Road goods yard (**108**) opened in 1887. Turn right into Hooper Street and follow the road to its end where it meets Leman Street.

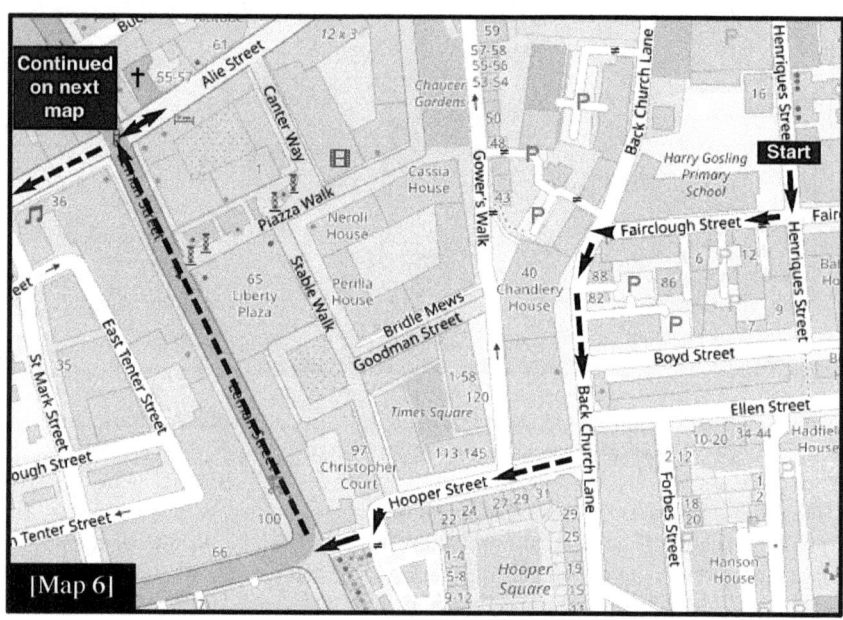

On the way you will pass the old pump house on your left (**legal.worked.sample**) [**45**]. This was built by the railway between 1886 and 1887 to power the hoists, capstans, and cranes at the goods yard. The ground floor contained a large boiler while above was the engine room. You might think that the building resembles a small church or chapel, and you would be right for it was constructed on the site of a former German Lutheran chapel, and so the building design is no accident.

Facing you on the right-hand-side of Hooper Street is an ornate door with two crests (**lush.single.mobile**) [46]. This building was owned by the railway, with the crests signifying that the railway went from the City of London to the coast at

Southend-on-Sea. You will also observe the back of a tall building with a clock tower adjacent to this door **[47]**. This is the Grade II listed Sugar House (now luxury flats) which contains a quarter-sized working replica of Big Ben (**reject.thus.tells**). More correctly it was the London headquarters of the Co-operative Wholesale Society and it was from here, between 1885 and the late 1960s, that sugar, tea, and coffee were stored prior to them being transported to its national headquarters in Manchester. Turn right into Leman Street, pass the front entrance of the Sugar House above which is the motto 'Labor and Wait' (with the American spelling of 'labor' being used on purpose to show support for the anti-slavery campaign).

A little further up on the left-hand-side of the road is Leman Street police station (**doors.guess.these**) **[48]**. It was here that James Sadler was taken and interviewed following his arrest **(85)**, and along with Commercial Street and Bishopsgate police stations was at the centre of operations during the Jack the Ripper investigations. The uninviting, faceless 1969 building stands on the same site as the 1849 police station, which itself was erected on the site of the Garrick Theatre and Jew's Temporary Shelter. It is still a police station, although closed to the public since 1995, and is a base for firearms officers and other specialist teams.

Continue your walk up Leman Street and on your right at Piazza Walk you will see a series of horse sculptures (**ramp.supply.crowned**) **[49]**. These are 'The Goodman's Fields Horses' (6 bronze life and quarter size horses) sculpted by Hamish Mackie. In the 16th century, the land here was farmed by Roland Goodman, whose son went on to let out the fields for the grazing of horses.

At the next intersection you will turn left into Alie Street, but note St. George's German Lutheran Church close to the junction if you had turned right instead (**levels.friday.chins**) **[50]**. Opened in 1762 this is the oldest surviving German

Church in the country. German speakers congregated in this part of London as they ran most of the sugar refining industry, which at the time was based around Aldgate (as evidenced by Sugar House that you passed earlier).

Also at the corner is The Eastern Dispensary building dating from 1858 (**indoor.sling.year**) **[51]**. Italianate in design it was 'Supported by Voluntary Contributions' with the aim of providing medicines free of charge to the poor of the area. It remained in use until World War II, and today is a public house, but one which has restored the building to its former glory with a mezzanine gallery overlooking the former consulting room.

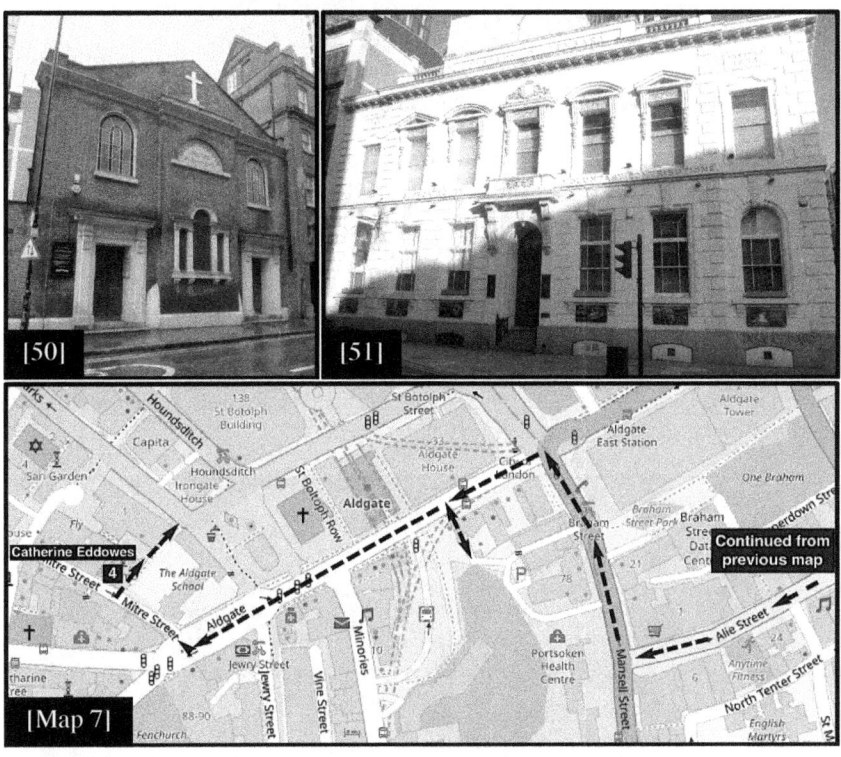

At the end of Alie Street [**Map 7**] turn right in Mansell Street and follow this road to where it meets Aldgate High Street where you will turn left. It was in Aldgate High Street that Catherine Eddowes was found drunk and taken into custody by Police Constable Louis Robinson on the evening of her murder (**34**).

Note the City of London dragon boundary marker (**ankle.soap.take**) [**52**] at the opposite side of the junction (**90**). On your left-hand-side as you turn the corner is the Hoop and Grapes public house at No. 47 Aldgate High Street (**crazy.unity.ramp**) [**53**]. It claims to be the oldest licensed public house in the City of London with its foundations dating back to the 13th century. The present leaning building with its timber-framed windows could date from as early as the 16th century. It is said that there once was a tunnel in the cellars (now sealed) which extended as far as the Tower of London. A quirk of this establishment was that there was a listening tube connecting the bars and cellars, through which the landlord could eavesdrop on conversations.

Just past the Hoop and Grapes is a passage (Little Somerset Street) which leads to an equally interesting public house, the Still and Star (**jolly.talent.double**) [54]. It dates from 1820 and is the sole survivor of what is termed a 'slum pub' i.e. one converted from a private house. Little Somerset Street was formerly Harrow Alley, but always known colloquially as Blood Alley. This was due to the large number butchers/slaughter houses in the vicinity which grew up here since if cattle on their way to Smithfield Market were slaughtered before entering the City of London no toll was payable. The name of the public house refers to a still that was housed in the hayloft of the building, while the star in question is the Star of David so emphasising the high Jewish presence in the area. Little has changed since Gustave Doré drew the public house in 1869 **(10)** [55]. If Jack the Ripper had been a butcher in the East End then he would almost certainly have known this establishment.

Retrace your steps to Aldgate High Street and turn left. The next point of interest is Aldgate Underground station on your right-hand-side (**rubble.reveal.cakes**) [56]. It was opened in 1876 and built over the plague pit adjacent to St. Botolph's church with the consequence that over 1,000 (out of a total of 5,136) bodies had to be moved. The station frontage (comprising green marble, pink granite, a glass canopy, leaded light windows, ornamental lamp brackets, and a frieze with lettering and the Metropolitan Railway monogram) dates from 1926, but the train shed behind is original. On the 7th July 2005 it was as a train from Liverpool Street was approaching the station that a suicide bomber detonated a device that killed 7 passengers.

The adjacent St. Botolph's church (**wage.rail.fired**) [57] dates from 1744, though much of the interior is late Victorian. It is one of 4 St. Botolph churches built during the 10th and 11th centuries close to the main gates of the City of London. The original Aldgate church belonged to the Knighten Guild which in 1115 gave the church to the newly established Priory of Holy Trinity, who promptly rebuilt it. In 1532 at the time of the dissolution of the monasteries it became the property of the Crown, and by 1740 was considered an unsafe structure. A new church was built at a cost of £5,536 2s. 5d. in 1744, and it was during this construction that the body of a boy was found in a standing position in one of the vaults. He was put on display with visitors paying 2d. to have a look. Apparently, people were very impressed by his well-preserved intestines. Daniel Defoe, the author of *Robinson Crusoe*, was married here in 1683, while Jeremy Bentham, the social reformer, was christened here in 1747. The Renatus Harris organ dating from 1676 is the oldest in London. Note the water fountain next to the church (**hired.upon.flags**) [**58**]. It was placed here by the Metropolitan Drinking Fountain (and Cattle Trough) Association whose aim it was to provide free drinking water for humans and animals (mainly horses) in urban environments. The first such fountain was established in 1859, and by 1867 there were some 800 fountains all over the country, but often found close to public houses or churchyards. This one dates from the 6th January 1905.

Adjacent to the church is the Sir John Cass's Foundation Primary School (**passes.rabble.valid**) **[59]**. The Foundation started in 1669 with money provided by Sir Samuel Stamp for the education of 40 boys (known as bluecoat boys on account of their uniform **[60]**) and 30 girls. In 1710 Alderman Sir John Cass agreed to provide further money, but died suddenly of a brain haemorrhage before he could sign the endowment deed – literally being found with a blood-stained quill at his desk. As a consequence, in 1738 the school closed for 10 years until the Chancery enforced the deed. The school moved to its current location in 1908 **[61]** & **[62]**, and to this day on Founder's Day each year all the pupils are given pens, stained red, which they wear in their lapels in memory of the tragic death of their benefactor.

Take the next right turn which is Mitre Street, and follow the school perimeter wall as it goes into Mitre Square. It was here in the southwest corner (**bucket.leap.object**) **[63]** that Police Constable Edward Watkins found the body of Catherine Eddowes (**35-36**). Follow the wall which will take you into St. James's Passage. In 1888 this was Church Passage, and at its end (**edge.exchanges.branded**) **[64]** is where Catherine Eddowes was last sighted at 1.35 a.m. as she talked with a man (almost certainly Jack the Ripper).

☙ 5 ☙
MARY KELLY - MILLER'S COURT
⇐ 30 minutes ⇒

At the end of St. James's passage turn left into Dukes Place [**Map 8**]. Soon this road becomes Bevis Marks where under a covered way on the left-hand-side you will see a gate and an opening. This is the entrance to Bevis Marks Synagogue (**others.wing.onion**) **[65]**, which having been founded in 1657 is the oldest in

London (and was originally used by Spanish and Portuguese Jews). The current building dates from 1701.

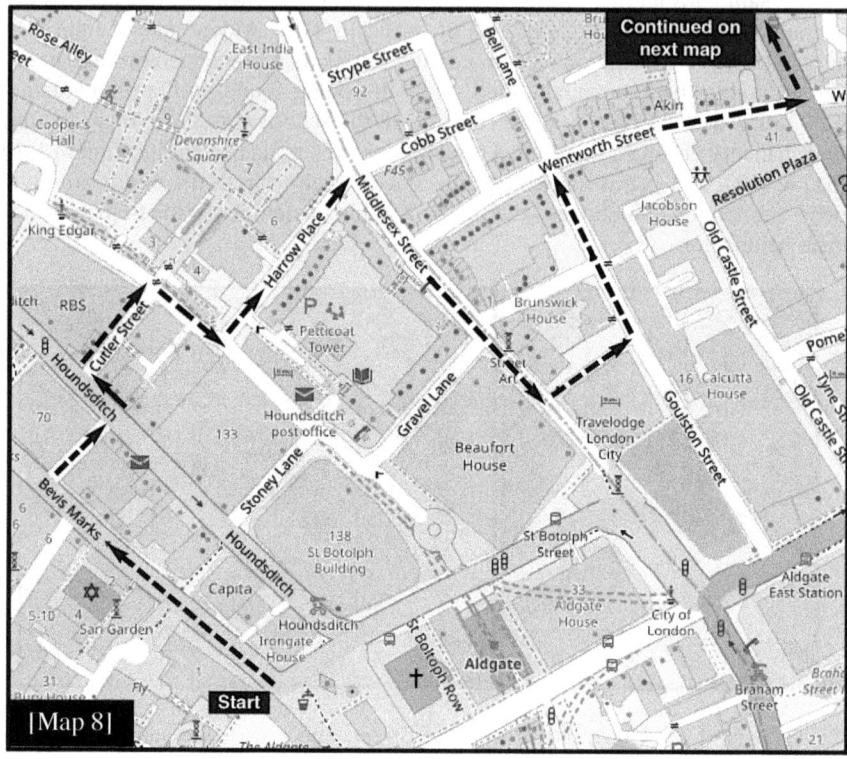

[Map 8]

The street name is a corruption of Burics Marks, the town house of the Abbot of Bury St. Edmunds which once stood here. Take the next right turn into Goring Street, and at the end turn left into Houndsditch (where the Whitechapel Bell Foundry was originally established (**20**)), and then the first right turn into Cutler Street. Note the coat of arms at the far end on the right-hand-side (**charge.people.adding**) [66]. This belongs to the Worshipful Company of Cutlers who actually have their livery hall at Warwick Lane in the City of London. Facing you at the end of Cutler Street you will see a small plaque at ground level which commemorates the 3 police officers who lost their lives in what became known as the Houndsditch Murders (**jeeps.year.casual**) [67]. The loss of life occurred when anarchists tried to break into a jeweller's shop at No. 119 Houndsditch on the 16th December 1910 – at the time it was the largest loss of police officers in a single night.

Turn right, which is still Cutler Street, and then left into Harrow Place. At the end of this road turn right into Middlesex Street. Up until around 1830 this was Petticoat Lane (**53**) and known for its street market (which sold old clothes predominantly). Even though the street name changed people still refer to the market, which takes place here every Sunday morning, as the Petticoat Lane Market [**68**]. Today the 1,000 plus stalls have spread out into the surrounding streets and still sell fashion and second-hand clothing. The part of the market located in Wentworth Street is open 6 days a week. You will go past Wentworth Street (which will be on your left-hand-side) and proceed to the next left turn which is New Goulston Street. Go along here to the end, and turn left into Goulston Street itself. On the opposite side of the street you will see the Model Dwellings where the so named 'Goulston Street Graffito' was found (**38-39**) (**crib.hoot.hurry**).

Continue up Goulston Street to its junction with Wentworth Street. Turn right into Wentworth Street. Again, you may like to compare the present street with that which Gustave Doré drew in 1869 (**9**). When you reach the junction with Commercial Street turn left into Commercial Street [**Map 9**].

149

Jack the Ripper Walks

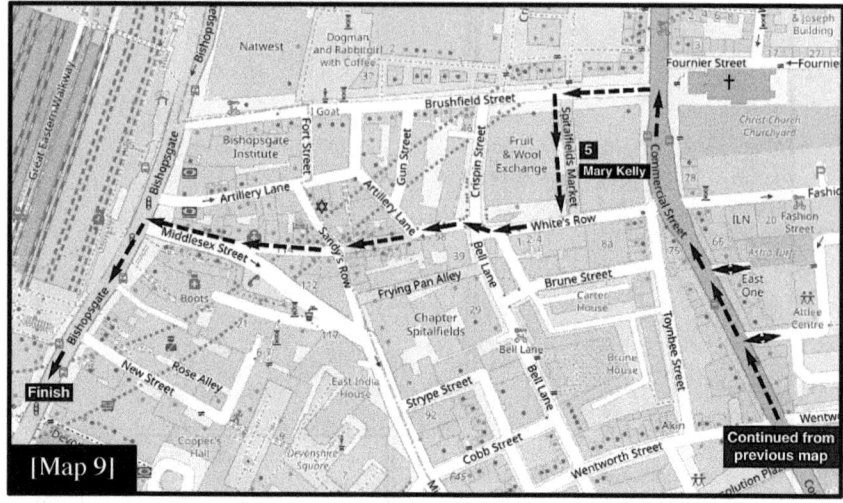

[Map 9]

On the right-hand-side of the road you will first come to Thrawl Street (**potato.civic.from**). This is the only section of this street to have survived in its original location – in the distance you might be able to make out the passage that leads to the Frying Pan public house that you walked down earlier (**135**). The next turning on the right is Lolesworth Close (**skirt.calls.locker**). This was Flower and Dean Street (**31**) with the location of the lodging house where Elizabeth Stride resided being just past the iron gates on the left-hand-side.

[69]   [70]

150

The next street up is Fashion Street and if you look up at the corner you will note that this was the location of the former Queen's Head public house **(later.squad.puddles)** [69] which would have been known by all the Jack the Ripper victims. As you continue up Commercial Street it should look familiar for in front of you on the right-hand-side is Christ Church and beyond the Ten Bells public house you visited earlier in the walk (**130**). However, before you reach there, you should observe the water fountain on your right-hand-side **(system.relay.castle)** [70]. It is in line with the fountain that Dorset Street extended from Commercial Street (on the opposite side of the road) to Crispin Street, and where Mary Kelly was murdered at Miller's Court (**45**). The location is still accessible today by turning left into Brushfield Street (opposite the Ten Bells public house), and on the left-hand-side of the London Fruit Exchange [**71**] there is a public right of way through to White's Row (**chops.birds.brain**). The location of No. 13 Miller's Court is in the atrium of the building (**kicked.same.taking**).

But, before you walk through the London Fruit Exchange building, look around you. You will note that just as in 1888 Christ Church still dominates the area, and Brushfield Street in particular [72]. If you look to the opposite side of the road you will see the City of London crest over the entrance to the old Spitalfields Market [73]. This is because in 1920 the Corporation of the City of London acquired and ran the market despite it being outside the City of London. Since, 2005 when the area was redeveloped the market is now owned by a private company (Ashenazy Acquisations). Part of the area's redevelopment included a 'beautification' of the streets in the form of new public works of art – one such installation, almost opposite where you are standing, is that of a wooden boat carrying 7 wire-mesh people [74]. It is the work of Greek artist and filmmaker Kalliopi Lemos, and is, rather unimaginatively, entitled *Wooden Boat with Seven People*. It is part of a series of artworks, *Navigating the Dark*, with the boat having been used to transport refugees from Turkey to Greece, and is thus a poignant reminder of the various waves of migrants who have come to this area in search of better lives over the centuries.

From the atrium and to your right if you have your back to Spitalfields Market, would have been Little Paternoster Row where Mary Kelly once lodged (**45**). This small thoroughfare ran from Dorset Street to Brushfield Street. Continue through the building to the other side where it meets White's Row. Turn right along White's Row to the end of the street where the imposing Lilian Knowles House (**monks.driven.feared**) dominates the far side of the road (slightly to your right) [75].

In the Footsteps of Jack the Ripper

This building was the former Providence Row night shelter (**12**) with, you will note, separate entrances for the male and female 'guests'. Go down the side of the building (Artillery Lane (**52**)) and at the rear you will see that a portion of an original façade that has been preserved (**film.guitar.defeat**) [76]. However, do not bear right, but continue straight into Artillery Passage [77]. This is a good example of how narrow many of the streets were at the time of Jack the Ripper. At the far end keep going straight into Widegate Street, which in turn joins Middlesex Street which soon ends at the junction with Bishopsgate. Turn left here and a little way along on the same side of the road is Bishopsgate police station (**froth.scope.atom**) where Catherine Eddowes was taken to sober-up on the night of her murder (**34-35**).

Congratulations – you have now completed the walk and on the opposite side of the road you should see the entrance to Liverpool Street station (**apples.upgrading.tricks**) which provides easy access to all parts of London and beyond.

THE GRAND TOUR

Duration: 4-5 hours
Start: Whitechapel station   **Finish:** Mile End station

This tour covers not just the canonical 5 murders of Mary Nichols, Annie Chapman, Elizabeth Stride, Catherine Eddowes, and Mary Kelly (along with other associated places of interest along the way), but also the other 8 cases covered in the 'Genesis' and 'Return' chapters of this book. Because the locations are dispersed over a wider area it is not practical to visit them in a chronological order. Although most of tour is done on foot, covering several miles of flat terrain, it also necessitates travel by train and bus to Poplar and Mile End respectively. Given that all the sites in *The Canonical Five Walk* are also visited in *The Grand Tour*, to save replicating large chunks of text reference will be made to parts of the former walk that should be followed as they occur, though some repetition is inevitable.

🐾 1 🐾
MARY NICHOLS, DURWARD STREET
⬅15 minutes ➡

For this section of the tour follow the same instructions as in *The Canonical Five Walk* (**123-125**).

🐾 2 🐾
ANNIE CHAPMAN, HANBURY STREET
⬅20 minutes ➡

For this section of the tour follow the same instructions as in *The Canonical Five Walk* (**125-128**).

🐾 3 🐾
MARY KELLY, MILLER'S COURT
⬅30 minutes ➡

As you continue down Hanbury Street [**Map 10**] you will pass Hanbury Hall (**teeth.past.pushed**) **[18]**. Note the tiles embedded in the wall which are a reminder of the former Huguenot influence in the area **[19]**. It was built in 1719 as a small French Huguenot chapel, but over the years it became La Patente Church (1740), a German Lutheran Church (1787), and a United Free Methodists Church prior to becoming part of the Anglican Christ Church in 1887. Charles Dickens was no stranger to the building, using it for public readings of his works, and in 1888 it was here that the 'match girls' **(60)** held their strike meetings as they began their protest for better working conditions at the nearby Bryant and May factory in Bow.

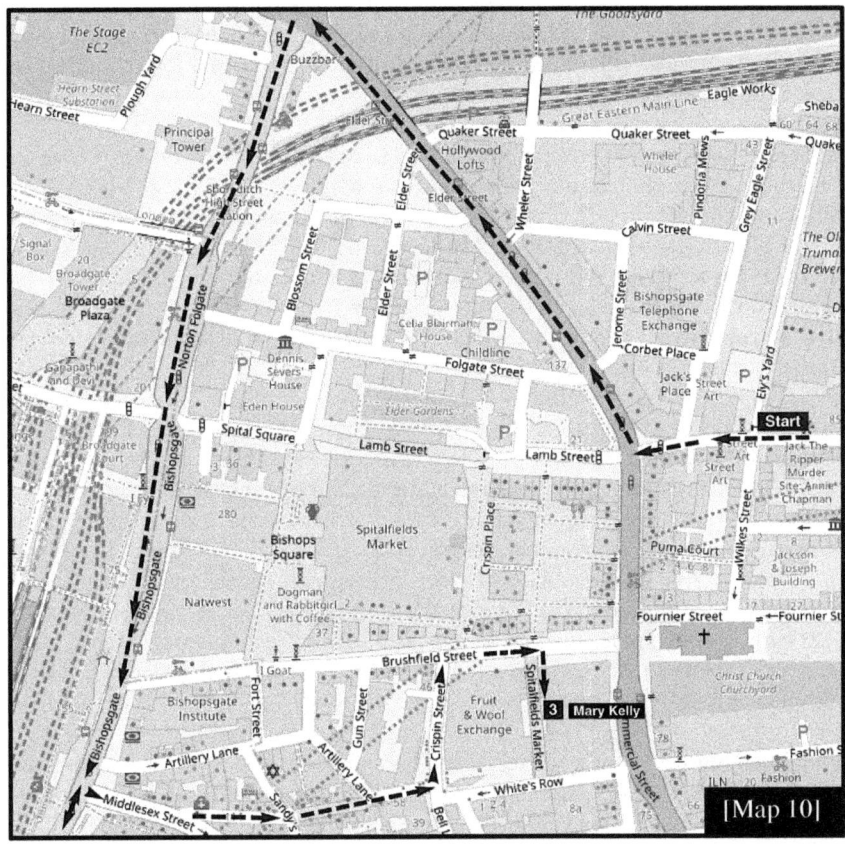

Continue on, and just past Wilkes Street on the left-hand-side is No. 12 Hanbury Street (**pushed.showed.longer**) which, as the blue plaque indicates, was where Bud Flanagan, the popular music hall and vaudeville entertainer, was born [**20**]. He was best known as part of the 'Crazy Gang', and as half the double act Flanagan and (Chesney) Allen in the 1930s to 1950s.

At the end of Hanbury Street is Commercial Street. Turn right and the next turning on the left will be Folgate Street on the corner of which is an imposing triangular-shaped building (**wonderfully.gazed.cowboy**) [**21**]. This is the very first Model Dwellings establishment opened by the Peabody Donation Fund in 1864 (**42**). Continue up to the next turning on the left (Fleur de Lis Street) and a similar styled building with Portland stone facing to the ground floor and set on a triangular piece of land can be seen (**loss.minute.pushed**) [22]. This was Commercial Street police station and dates from 1874 (with the upper storey not being added until 1906). Note the inscription '*dieu et mon droit*' above what was the main entrance [23]. Along with Leman Street and Bishopsgate it was one of the 3 key police stations during the Jack the Ripper investigations. Its most famous occupant was Detective Inspector Frederick Abberline.

Continue walking up Commercial Street, over the main railway line into Liverpool Street station, until you come to a major junction where you will turn left into Shoreditch High Street (A10). Walk down here passing Folgate Street, Spital Square, Brushfield Street, Artillery Lane, and Middlesex Street. You are now in Bishopsgate with Liverpool Street station to your right. Just past Middlesex Street you will come across Bishopsgate police station (**froth.scope.atom**) where Catherine Eddowes was taken to sober-up on the night of her murder (**34-35**).

Retrace your steps and go down Middlesex Street. Soon you will bear left into Widegate Street and then into Artillery Passage [77]. This is a good example of how narrow many of the streets were at the time of Jack the Ripper. Continue straight into Artillery Lane, and note on your left-hand-side an original façade that has been preserved (**film.guitar.defeat**) [76]. At the end of Artillery Lane where it meets Crispin Street is the imposing Lilian Knowles House (**monks.driven.feared**) [75]. This is the former Providence Row night shelter (**12**) with, you will note, separate entrances for the male and female 'guests'. Turn left into Crispin Street and follow the road to the end at which point you will turn right into Brushfield Street.

Immediately in front of you is Christ Church which, just as in 1888, dominates the area, and Brushfield Street in particular [72]. You should also note to your left the City of London crest over the entrance to the old Spitalfields Market [73]. This is because in 1920 the Corporation of the City of London acquired and ran the market despite it being outside the City of London. Since 2005, when the area was redeveloped, the market has been owned by a private company (Ashenazy Acquisitions). Part of the area's redevelopment included a 'beautification' of the streets in the form of new public works of art – one such installation, which you will soon pass on your left as you walk along Brushfield Street, is that of a wooden boat carrying 7 wire-mesh people [74]. It is the work of Greek artist and filmmaker Kalliopi Lemos, and is, rather unimaginatively, entitled *Wooden Boat with Seven People*. It is part of a series of artworks, *Navigating the Dark*, with the boat having been used to transport refugees from Turkey to Greece, and is thus a poignant reminder of the various waves of migrants who have come to this area in search of better lives over the centuries.

Just past here on your right is the London Fruit Exchange building (**chops.birds.brain**) **[71]** where there is a public right of way connecting to White's Row. This right of way will take you to the spot where Mary Kelly was killed at No. 13 Miller's Court (**45**) in Dorset Street (which ran parallel to Brushfield Street). Although Dorset Street no longer exists the location of her murder is as you enter the large atrium (**kicked.same.taking**). To the right of the atrium if you have your back to Spitalfields Market, would have been Little Paternoster Row where Mary Kelly once lodged (**45**). This small thoroughfare ran between Dorset Street and Brushfield Street.

❧ 4 ❧
ANNIE MILLWOOD, WHITE'S ROW
⇐2 minutes ⇒

Continue through the London Fruit Exchange building until it emerges in White's Row (**58**) [**Map 11**]. In front of you slightly to the right is No. 5 White's Row (**price.bets.state**), a fine example of an original Georgian merchant's residence built between 1724 and 1743 [**78**]. Internally it has been redesigned to incorporate 5-bedrooms, 5-bathrooms, 3-living rooms, a study, and a roof terrace – in 2020 it was up for sale at an asking price of £13,770 per square metre of living space. To your left is No. 8 White's Row (**asleep.swung.shakes**). This is the location of where Spitalfields Chambers once stood, and where Annie Millwood lived at the time of her death (**57**).

☙ 5 ☙
EMMA SMITH, BRICK LANE
⇐25 minutes ⇒

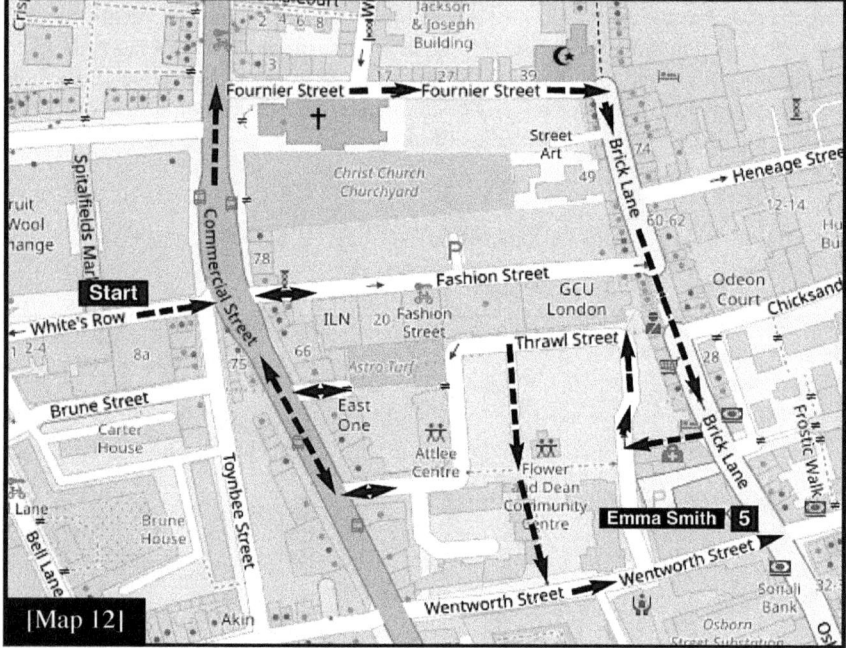

[Map 12]

Continue to the end of White's Row [**Map 12**]. Immediately in front of you on the opposite the corner you will note that this was the location of the former Queen's Head public house (**later.squad.puddles**) [69] which would have been known by all the Jack the Ripper victims. Turn right into Commercial Street. The first turn on your left-hand-side is Lolesworth Close (**skirt.calls.locker**). This was formerly Flower and Dean Street (**31**). The location of the lodging house where Elizabeth Stride resided would have been just beyond the iron gates on the left-hand-side. Continue on down Commercial Street to the next turning on your left, Thrawl Street (**potato.civic.from**). This is the only section of this street to have survived in its original location – in the distance you might be able to make out a passage that leads to the Frying Pan public house, a location you will visit later in this tour (**135**).

From here you should retrace your steps to Fashion Street (where the Queen's Head public house is on the corner). Fashion Street itself was laid out in the middle of the 17th century and was originally called Fossan Street after brothers Thomas and Lewis who owned large portions of land here. It later became corrupted to Fashion Street so its name has nothing to do with the clothing industry as many assume. It was an address in Fashion Street that Catherine Eddowes falsely gave as her abode to the police when released from Bishopsgate police station on the night of her murder (**35**). The arcade on the south side of the street [**33**] dates from 1905 and was the idea of Abraham Davis who intended to build 2 such covered structures with cross-passages that would contain 250 small shops. In the end only 63 were finished and by 1909 he had gone bankrupt.

Continue going up Commercial Street and very soon on the right-hand-side you will come to a water fountain (**system.relay.castle**) [**70**]. It is in line with the fountain that Dorset Street extended from Commercial Street (on the opposite side of the road) to Crispin Street, and where Mary Kelly was murdered at Miller's Court (**45**) – a location visited earlier in this tour.

You should now be able to see Christ Church and the Ten Bells public house in front of you. The Ten Bells (**tunes.ridge.coins**) [**26**] is where Mary Kelly was seen drinking with Elizabeth Foster on the night of her murder (**45**), but this popular drinking hole would have been known by all the victims of Jack the Ripper. It was established in 1755 (as the Eight Bells) adjacent to where it now stands, and moved to its current location in 1851 when Commercial Street was cut. The name refers to the peel of bells at Christ Church which until 1788 had just 8 bells, then 10 bells, and finally an even dozen. However, in 1836 there was a fire at the church which reduced that number by 4. Hence, the public house should more accurately revert to its original name. The interior is pure Victorian with some original blue and white floral pattern tiling, and a mural entitled *Spitalfields in ye Olden Time – visiting a Weaver's Shop* thus commemorating the weaving heritage of the area. This premises has always been a magnet for Jack the Ripper enthusiasts, and it even featured in a scene of the 1999 film *From Hell* in which Detective Inspector Frederick Abberline (played by Johnny Depp) has a drink with Mary Kelly.

As you have already noted earlier in the tour, the whole area of Spitalfields is dominated by Nicholas Hawksmoor's Christ Church [**27**] built between 1714 and 1729 to show an Anglican presence in a predominantly Huguenot part of London. In time the Huguenots too would come to worship here as is evident by the number of gravestones with French names in the graveyard. The nave [**28**] was described as being a very plain rectangular box albeit with Composite order columns, a richly decorated flat ceiling, and clerestory to allow natural lighting. Looking at this magnificent building in 2020 it is hard to believe that in 1960 the church was nearly derelict and in urgent need of restoration. The crypt became a rehabilitation

centre for homeless alcoholic men until 2000. Today it has disabled access which leads to a café which is open to the public and is highly recommended.
On the opposite side of the road to Christ Church and the Ten Bells are entrances to Spitalfields Market **[25]** which has been trading since 1638. Originally for the sale of 'flesh, fowl and roots', today it is popular for fashion, arts and crafts, and general goods. There are several food outlets as well as public toilets. You may like to explore the market further, or take a break at the Ten Bells.

From here you should turn right into Fournier Street and proceed along its full length to Brick Lane. The street, with its Georgian townhouses, has changed little since the 1720s when it became a fashionable road for Huguenots involved with the silk trade **[29]**. Originally called Church Street, it was renamed after one such Huguenot, George Fournier, while currently one of its most celebrated residents is another George, George Passmore who lives here with fellow artist Gilbert Proesch. You might like to note that the numbering of at least one property is very Harry Potteresque (**grow.silks.target**)**[30]**.

Turn right into Brick Lane (**64**) and almost immediately you will see the blue plaque at No. 55 commemorating the family home of Haroon Shamsher, founder of Joi, an alternative dub/dance music DJ team he set up with his brother Farook (**kinds.mini.boat**) **[31]**. A little further along, and also on the right-hand-side, is Christ Church School which dates from 1873 (**solve.slips.arch**) **[32]**.

The next street down on the right-hand-side is again Fashion Street (**clean.tanks.surely**), and it is here that many seeking out the locations of Jack the Ripper can become confused for the street layouts have changed almost beyond recognition since 1888, though the street names have been retained. Between here and Wentworth Street (which is the next street down on the right) used to be Flower and Dean Street, and Thrawl Street running parallel to each other, while running across these 2 roads and intersecting with Wentworth Street was George Street (where Mary Kelly (**45**), and Emma Smith (**62**) may both have lived for a while). However, there is an anomaly here since maps dating from 1860 and 1900 show George Street ending at Flower and Dean Street, whereas intermediate maps from 1890 show it running through to Fashion Street. It should also be noted that by 1900 George Street had become Lolesworth Street. Another problem arises as there were no fewer than 3 George Streets in the area: to the east of Brick Lane and running parallel to the one that became Lolesworth Street was the 2nd George Street, but this road was renamed Casson Street in 1883, while the final George Street was closer to Commercial Road and the St. George Brewery (and is, in fact, the one in which Mary Kelly lodged).

Proceed down Brick Lane. The next turning on your left is Chicksand Street (named after a village in Bedfordshire). It was opposite here (by No. 25 Brick

Lane (**chart.sock.melon**)) that Flower and Dean Street connected with Commercial Street. Today behind these modern flats is Thrawl Street. This is because when the new estate was built Thrawl Street was designated to run around the perimeter forming the shape of an upside-down toilet 'U' bend. Carry on down Brick Lane a little further until just before the iron arch over the street.

Here on the right-hand-side you will find an Indian restaurant (**spoken.planet.olive**) [34]. If you look up you will see the original name of this establishment was The Frying Pan, the public house where Mary Nichols was seen just prior to her murder (18). At the side of the building is an alley which you should go down [35]. It is the alley that you saw when you passed the other end of Thrawl Street earlier in the tour. This was the original Thrawl Street which connected with Commercial Street (which can be seen in the distance). It was in this street that Mary Nichols resided (18), and from where, shortly before her demise, she was ejected for not having sufficient funds to pay for her night's accommodation. It is also the street in which Mary Kelly resided for a short time (45), and in which direction she was heading when approached by Jack the Ripper (47). Frances Coles also lodged in Thrawl Street (84), and just a few hours before her murder had asked her landlady if she could return there if she paid her rent arrears. Later that same evening her man friend, James Sadler, was mugged here (85).

At the end of the alley turn right (which is also Thrawl Street) and just follow the road around the corner (still Thrawl Street) [36]. As you turn the corner you are now approximately where Flower and Dean Street was located. Elizabeth Stride resided in a common lodging house at No. 32 Flower and Dean Street (29), while Catherine Eddowes was further up the road at No. 55 (34). Immediately before her encounter with Jack the Ripper in Thrawl Street, Mary Kelly was spotted by George Hutchinson in Flower and Dean Street (47). Another person spotted in this road on the night of their death was Alice McKenzie (77).

Half way along this section of road you will see Flower and Dean Walk on your left [37]. Go into Flower and Dean Walk (which would have been George Street, and latterly Lolesworth Street) and walk to the far end which is the intersection with Wentworth Street.

You will have just passed under a brick arch (**plus.sports.level**) which was the former entrance to the Rothschild Buildings in Flower and Dean Street [38]. It was relocated here as a reminder of those model dwellings which were erected by the Four Per Cent Industrial Dwelling Company Ltd. in 1886 (42). There is another reminder of the past if you look up and down Wentworth Street [39] and compare it to the picture on page 9 of how the road appeared to Gustave Doré in 1869.

Turn left along Wentworth Street until it comes to the intersection with Brick Lane on your left, and Osborn Street to your right. The building to your left on the corner, No. 1 Brick Lane [**79**], occupies the site of the former chocolate factory, and although the killing of Emma Smith was known as the Osborn Street murder her body, according to police reports, was found opposite No. 10 Brick Lane by the railings of the cocoa factory (**swept.gives.flying**) (**62-64**).

⁘ 6 ⁘
MARTHA TABRAM, GEORGE YARD BUILDINGS
⇐10 minutes ⇒

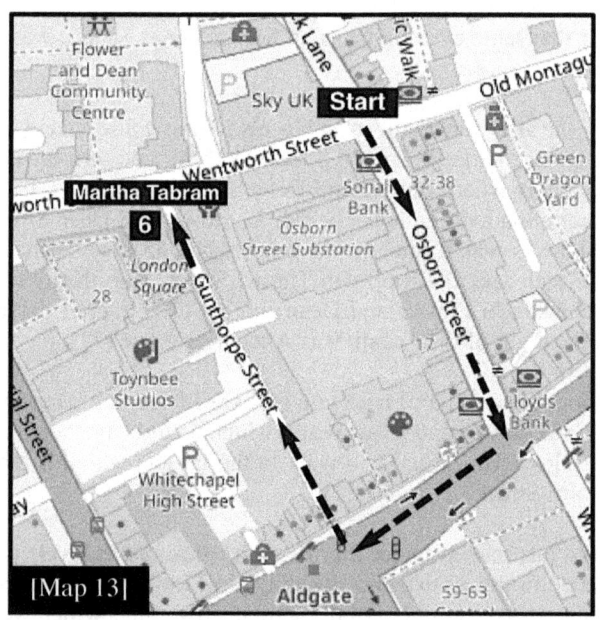

Turn right [**Map 13**] into Osborn Street and go down to the end of the road to where it meets Whitechapel High Street. On the corner you will note Jack the Chipper take away (**local.settle.skinny**) [**40**]. The last sighting of Mary Nichols was at the intersection with the main road (**erase.data.leaned**) and it was here she talked with fellow prostitute Emily Holland (**19**).

Turn right and note the blue plaque (**poster.buck.awards**) [**80**] to Isaac Rosenberg as you come to the Whitechapel Art Gallery (known today as simply the Whitechapel Gallery). Rosenberg was born in Bristol but brought up in the East End, and is perhaps best-known for his 'Trench Poems' written during World War I, as well as his play *The Unicorn*. He died in 1918 while on active service. Also look up and you will see what appears to be a man on a horse riding backwards while reading a book [**81**]. It is Rodney Graham's weather vane commissioned to commemorate the expansion of the art gallery into the former Passmore Edwards library and is, in fact, supposed to depict an artist in the guise of a 16th century humanist scholar.

A little further along is the main entrance to the Whitechapel Gallery (**twice.shelf.watch**) [**82**] which is free to enter. It was opened in 1901 with the aim of exhibiting the works of contemporary artists and hosting special displays that have an interest to the local community. Not far from here on your right-hand-side, close to a large tree, you will see the narrow passageway between 2 shops that is Gunthorpe Street (**full.stages.funded**). There are tiles on the wall indicating both the street and local attractions. Enter the alley which soon opens up into Gunthorpe Street proper. On your left-hand-side is Canon Barnett Primary School built in 1901 (**think.improving.courier**) [83]. It is named after a former vicar of St. Jude's Church on Commercial Street, who, with the help of a £6,000 donation from Passmore Edwards (who built the Whitechapel Library that you passed earlier), was able to purchase land and build the Whitechapel Art Gallery. As you reach the end of the street look out for the Broadway block of flats which stand where George Yard Buildings once stood, and where Martha Tabram was murdered (**change.layers.waddled**) (**65-71**).

⦿ 7 ⦿
ALICE MCKENZIE, CASTLE ALLEY
⇐10 minutes ⇒

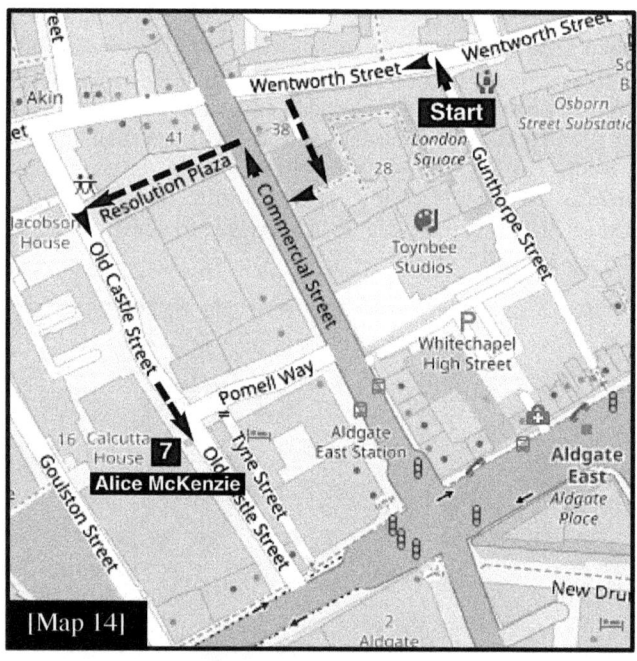

From the top of Gunthorpe Street [**Map 14**] turn left into Wentworth Street. You may like to compare the present street with that which Gustave Doré drew in 1869 (**9**).

In the Footsteps of Jack the Ripper

Just before the major junction with Commercial Street there is an alley on your left that you should take. It leads to the redeveloped Toynbee Hall complex (**assure.clubs.hangs**) [**84**], part of which contains a free exhibition telling the stories of social action from the world's first university settlement (**70-71**). Note the blue plaque dedicated to Dr. Jimmy Mallon who was a warden here, and also the clock tower [**85**] (which was damaged by bombing during World War II) in the corner. If facing the clock tower turn right and exit to Commercial Street. On the opposite side of Commercial Street, and slightly to your right, you will see Resolution Plaza. Cross the road and walk down Resolution Plaza which goes between 2 new housing developments. At the far end turn left into Old Castle Street. Soon on the right-hand-side you will pass the remaining façade of the 1846 wash houses (**submit.comb.atom**) (**79**). Just pass here on the same side of the road the body of Alice McKenzie was found by Police Constable Walter Andrews (**level.shaky.calls**) (**77**).

⋅⋅ 8 ⋅⋅
CATHERINE EDDOWES, MITRE SQUARE
⇐15 minutes ⇒

Walk to the bottom of Old Castle Street [**Map 15**] and turn right into Whitechapel High Street. Take the next right turn into Goulston Street. Proceed up this street and towards the top end you will pass through a barrier at the junction with New Goulston Street. The next building to your right is the Model Dwellings where the so named 'Goulston Street Graffito' was found (**38-39**) (**crib.hoot.hurry**).

Retrace your steps and go down New Goulston Street which will now be on your right. At the end turn right into Middlesex Street. Up until around 1830 this was Petticoat Lane (**53**) and known for its street market (which sold old clothes predominantly). Even though the street name changed people still refer to the market, which takes place here every Sunday morning, as the Petticoat Lane Market **[68]**. Today the 1,000 plus stalls have spread out into the surrounding streets and still sell fashion and second-hand clothing. Walk up Middlesex Street until you reach Harrow Place on your left. Go down Harrow Place to its end where you will turn right into Cutler Street. Soon Cutler Street bears left with the continuation of the road being Devonshire Square. Look to your right and at ground level affixed to the wall next to the street sign you will see a small plaque which commemorates the 3 police officers who lost their lives in what became known as the Houndsditch Murders (**jeeps.year.casual**) **[67]**. The loss of life occurred when anarchists tried to break into a jeweller's shop at No. 119 Houndsditch on the 16th December 1910 – at the time it was the largest loss of police officers in a single night.

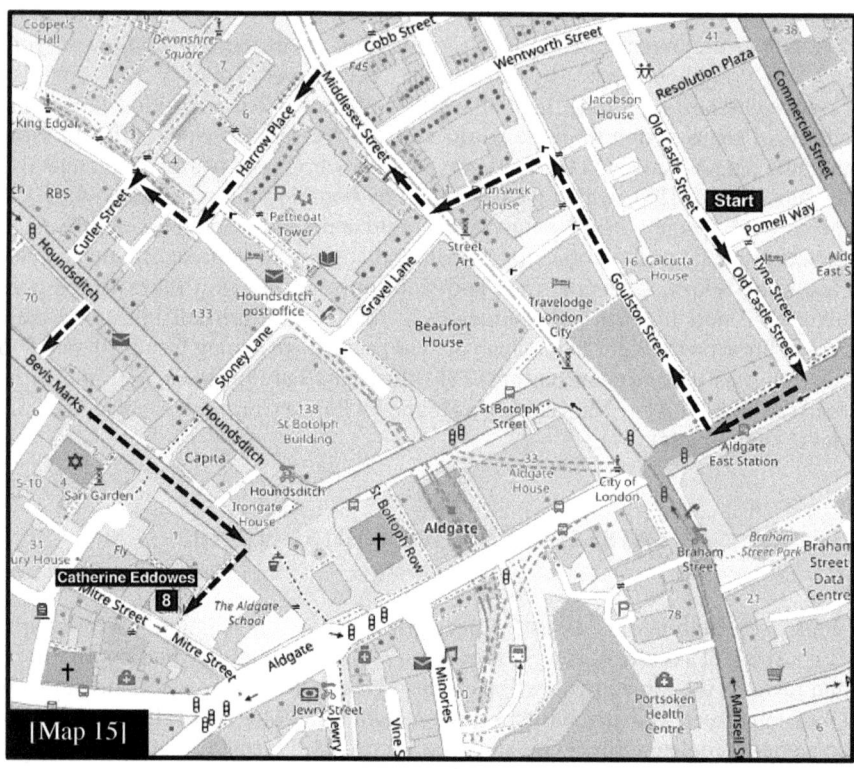

[Map 15]

As you bear left along Cutler Street note the coat of arms on the left-hand-side (**charge.people.adding**) **[66]**. This belongs to the Worshipful Company of Cutlers who actually have their livery hall at Warwick Lane in the City of London. At the next junction turn left into Houndsditch (where the Whitechapel Bell

Foundry was originally established (**20**)), and then the first left turn into Goring Street. At the end of this road turn left again into Bevis Marks where under a covered way on the right-hand-side, just past the junction with Bury Street, you will see a gate and an opening. This is the entrance to Bevis Marks Synagogue (**others.wing.onion**) [**65**], which having been founded in 1657 is the oldest in London (and was originally used by Spanish and Portuguese Jews). The current building dates from 1701. The street name is a corruption of Burics Marks, the town house of the Abbot of Bury St. Edmunds which once stood here. As you continue down Bevis Marks it soon becomes Dukes Place and will bear to the left. However, at the corner on the right-hand-side is St. James's Passage which you should walk down. In 1888 this was Church Passage, and at it is here (**edge.exchanges.branded**) [**64**] that Catherine Eddowes was last sighted at 1.35 a.m. as she talked with a man (almost certainly Jack the Ripper). The passage goes into Mitre Square where soon afterwards Police Constable Edward Watkins found the body of Catherine Eddowes (**35-36**) in the southwest corner (**bucket.leap.object**) [**63**].

🐾 9 🐾
ELIZABETH STRIDE, HENRIQUES STREET
⇐25 minutes ⇒

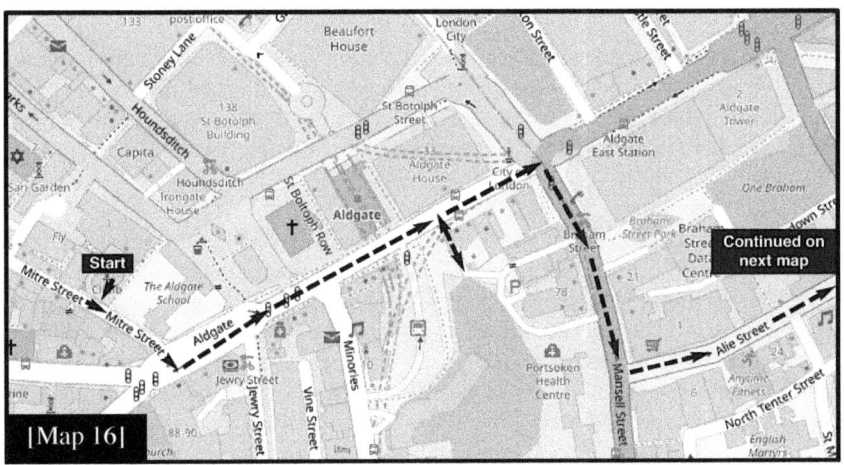

[Map 16]

Follow the wall on your left [**Map 16**] to the far side of Mitre Square. At the corner it becomes Mitre Street and continues round to the left. Soon you will reach Aldgate High Street where you should turn left again still following the same wall, which you will now note forms the perimeter of the Sir John Cass's Foundation Primary School whose main entrance is in Aldgate Square to your left (**passes.rabble.valid**) [**59**]. The Foundation started in 1669 with money provided by Sir Samuel Stamp for the education of 40 boys (known as bluecoat boys on account of their uniform [**60**]) and 30 girls. In 1710 Alderman Sir John Cass [**60**] agreed to provide further money, but died suddenly of a brain haemorrhage before he could sign the endowment deed – literally being found with a blood-stained quill at his desk. As a consequence, the school closed in 1738 for 10 years until the Chancery enforced the deed. The school moved to its current location in 1908 [**61**] & [**62**], and to this day on Founder's Day each year all the pupils are given pens, stained red, which they wear in their lapels in memory of the tragic death of their benefactor.

It was in Aldgate High Street that Catherine Eddowes was found drunk and taken into custody by Police Constable Louis Robinson on the evening of her murder (**34**). Continue straight and the next point of interest is the adjacent St. Botolph's church (**wage.rail.fired**) [**57**] which dates from 1744, though much of the interior is late Victorian. It is one of 4 St. Botolph churches built during the 10th and 11th centuries close to the main gates of the City of London. The original Aldgate church belonged to the Knighten Guild which in 1115 gave the church to the newly established Priory of Holy Trinity, who promptly rebuilt it. In 1532 at the time of the dissolution of the monasteries it became the property of the Crown, and by 1740 was considered an unsafe structure. A new church was built at a cost of £5,536 2s. 5d. in 1744, and it was during this construction that the body of a boy was found in a standing position in one of the vaults. He was put on display with visitors paying 2d. to have a look. Apparently, people were very impressed by his well-preserved intestines. Daniel Defoe, the author of *Robinson Crusoe*, was married here in 1683, while Jeremy Bentham, the social reformer, was christened here in 1747. The Renatus Harris organ dating from 1676 is the oldest in London.

Also note the water fountain just before the church (**hired.upon.flags**) [**58**]. It was placed here by the Metropolitan Drinking Fountain (and Cattle Trough) Association whose aim it was to provide free drinking water for humans and animals (mainly horses) in urban environments. The first such fountain was established in 1859, and by 1867 there were some 800 fountains all over the country, but often found close to public houses or churchyards. This one dates from the 6th January 1905.

A little further along and still on your left-hand-side is Aldgate Underground station (**rubble.reveal.cakes**) [**56**]. It was opened in 1876 and built over the plague pit adjacent to St. Botolph's church with the consequence that over 1,000 (out of a total of 5,136) bodies had to be moved. The station frontage (comprising green marble, pink granite, a glass canopy, leaded light windows, ornamental lamp brackets, and a frieze with lettering and the Metropolitan Railway monogram) dates from 1926, but the train shed behind is original. On the 7th July

2005 it was as a train from Liverpool Street was approaching the station that a suicide bomber detonated a device that killed 7 passengers.

You now need to cross the road at the pedestrian crossing and continue going along Aldgate High Street. Almost immediately you will come to an alley on your right-hand-side which leads to Little Somerset Street. Down here you will find the Still and Star public house (**jolly.talent.double**) [54]. It dates from 1820 and is the sole survivor of what is termed a 'slum pub' i.e. one converted from a private house. Little Somerset Street was formerly Harrow Alley, but always know colloquially as Blood Alley. This was due to the large number butchers/slaughter houses in the vicinity which grew up here since if cattle on their way to Smithfield Market were slaughtered before entering the City of London no toll was payable. The name of the public house refers to a still that was housed in the hayloft of the building, while the star in question is the Star of David so emphasising the high Jewish presence in the area. Little has changed since Gustave Doré drew the public house in 1869 **(10)** [55]. If Jack the Ripper had been a butcher in the East End then he would almost certainly have known this establishment.

Retrace your steps back to Aldgate High Street and turn right. On your right-hand-side you will see the Hoop and Grapes public house at No. 47 Aldgate High Street (**crazy.unity.ramp**) [53]. It claims to be the oldest licensed house in the City of London with its foundations dating back to the 13th century. The present leaning building with its timber-framed windows could date from as early as the 16th century. It is said that there once was a tunnel in the cellars (now sealed) which extended as far as the Tower of London. A quirk of this establishment was that there was a listening tube connecting the bars and cellars, through which the landlord could eavesdrop on conversations.

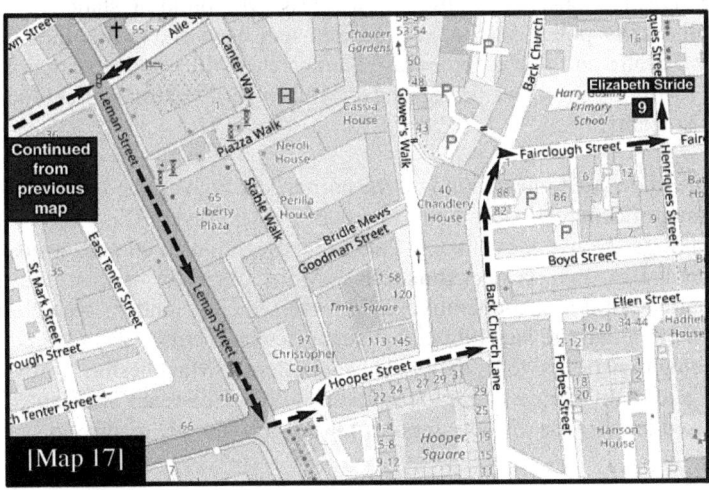

[Map 17]

Continue to the next junction, and turn right into Mansell Street, but before you do this look to the opposite side of the road to your left and you will see a City of London dragon boundary marker (**ankle.soap.take**) (**90**) [**52**]. The next left turn is Alie Street which you should take. Continue to the intersections with Leman Street [**Map 17**]. On the opposite left-hand corner is The Eastern Dispensary building dating from 1858 (**indoor.sling.year**) [**51**]. Italianate in design it was 'Supported by Voluntary Contributions' with the aim of providing medicines free of charge to the poor of the area. It remained in use until World War II, and today is a public house, but one which has restored the building to its former glory with a mezzanine gallery overlooking the former consulting room.

Also look just beyond the junction and on the left-hand-side is St. George's German Lutheran Church (**levels.friday.chins**) [**50**]. Opened in 1762 this is the oldest surviving German Church in the country. German speakers congregated in this part of London as they ran most of the sugar refining industry, which at the time was based around Aldgate.

Turn right and as you walk down Leman Street on your left at Piazza Walk you will see a series of horse sculptures (**ramp.supply.crowned**) [**49**]. These are 'The Goodman's Fields Horses' (6 bronze life and quarter size horses) sculpted by Hamish Mackie. In the 16th century, the land here was farmed by Roland Goodman, whose son went on to let out the fields for the grazing of horses.

A little further along, and on the right-hand-side of the road, is Leman Street police station (**doors.guess.these**) [**48**]. It was here that James Sadler was taken and interviewed following his arrest (**85**), and along with Commercial Street and Bishopsgate police stations was at the centre of operations during the Jack the Ripper investigations. The uninviting, faceless 1969 building stands on the same site as the 1849 police station, which itself had been erected on the site of the Garrick Theatre and Jew's Temporary Shelter. It is still a police station, although closed to the public since 1995, and is a base for firearms officers and other specialist teams.

Continue to the next intersection on the corner of which on the left-hand-side is a rather magnificent red-bricked building with a clock tower [**47**]. This is the Grade II listed Sugar House (now luxury flats) which contains a quarter-sized working replica of Big Ben (**reject.thus.tells**). More correctly it was the London headquarters of the Co-operative Wholesale Society and it was from here, between 1885 and the late 1960s, that sugar, tea, and coffee were stored prior to them being transported to its national headquarters in Manchester. Note the motto 'Labor and Wait' above the main entrance – the American spelling of 'labor' being used on purpose to show support for the anti-slavery campaign.

Turn left here into Hooper Street and facing you is the old pump house (**legal.worked.sample**) [45]. This was built by the London, Tilbury & Southend Railway between 1886 and 1887 to power the hoists, capstans, and cranes at the nearby goods yard. The ground floor contained a large boiler while above was the engine room. You might think that the building resembles a small church or chapel, and you would be right for it was constructed on the site of a former German Lutheran chapel, and so the building design is no accident. As the road bends look to your left and in the corner is an ornate door with two crests (**lush.single.mobile**) [46]. This building was also owned by the railway, with the crests signifying that the railway went from the City of London to the coast at Southend-on-Sea.

Follow Hooper Street to the end where it meets Back Church Lane. Turn left into this road and note the several fine Victorian former warehouses such as the one belonging to Charles Kinloch & Co. Limited (**invest.ahead.usage**) [44]. The warehouses were located here because they backed onto the London, Tilbury & Southend Railway's Commercial Road goods yard (**108**) opened in 1887. Take the next right turn into Fairclough Street and soon you will see the Harry Gosling Primary School on your left. You may like to note the mosaic celebrating 100 years of the school dating from 2010 (**plays.flood.death**) [43].

Turn first left into Henriques Street. Just past the first school gate (**enter.quest.tinsel**) would have been the entrance to Dutfield's Yard where the body of Elizabeth Stride was discovered (**29**). On the opposite side of the street is Bernhard Baron House, another reminder that the area was predominantly Jewish [42]. Note the plaque in memory of those members of the West London and Liberal Jewish Synagogue who gave their lives during World War I.

❧ 10 ❧
THE PINCHIN STREET TORSO, PINCHIN STREET
⇐ 10 minutes ⇒

Retrace your steps to Fairclough Street and turn left [**Map 18**]. At the end of the street turn right into Christian Street and walk down until you almost reach the railway bridge. No. 78 Christian Street was the home of the German Bakers' Club, which in 1898 was one of 4 premises to be raided by the police in search of illicit spirits being sold i.e. those on which tax had not been paid. The secretary of the club, Philip Schmidt, was found guilty of this activity and ordered to pay a fine of £125 – a substantial sum of money for the time. The club was raided a second time a few years later and this time Schmidt was ordered to pay £25 along with costs of 5 guineas.

The last turning on the right before the railway bridge is Pinchin Street. On the corner of Pinchin Street and Christian Street is a rather strange looking building (**silks.loser.dots**) **[86]**. It was actually constructed in 2007 out of 35 shipping containers to provide a doctor's surgery, office spec and a roof garden, but is now closed awaiting redevelopment.

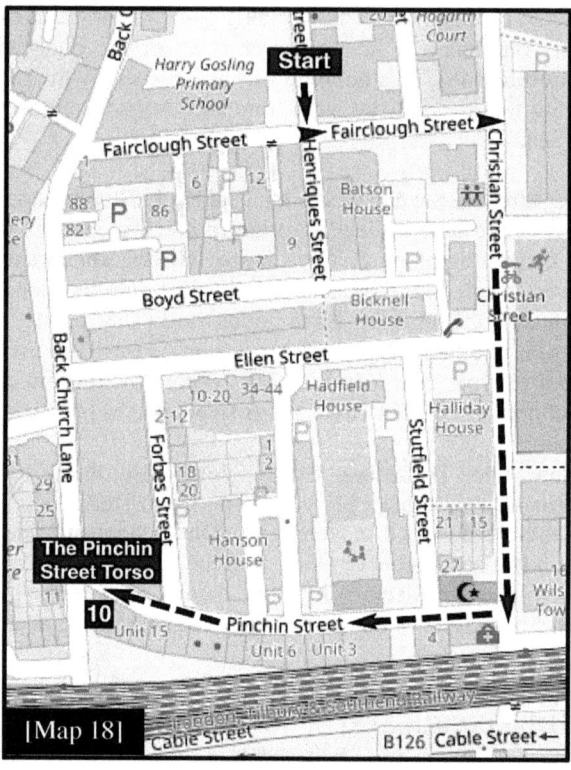

[Map 18]

Turn right into Pinchin Street. However, note that if you had continued under the railway bridge just the other side Christian Street comes to an end at Cable Street. It was at this junction on Sunday 4th October 1936 that anti-fascist groups built roadblocks to prevent Oswald Mosley's British Union of Fascists from marching through the East End. With an estimated 20,000 anti-fascists, 2,500 fascists, and 6,500 police officers on the scene violent clashes were inevitable in what became known as the Battle of Cable Street.

As you proceed along Pinchin Street you will note the various lock-up units under the railway arches which follow the curve of the old spur into the Commercial Road goods yard. If you follow the numbering when you reach No. 14 you have arrived at the spot where the Pinchin Street Torso was discovered by Police Constable William Penett on the 10th September 1889 (**glass.album.ended**) (**80**).

☙ 11 ☙
FRANCES COLES, SWALLOW GARDENS
⇐ 10 minutes ⇒

[86] [87]

Continue to the end of Pinchin Street [**Map 19**] and turn left into Back Church Lane. Go under the railway bridge to where the road comes to a T junction. Turn right into Cable Street with the railway to your right. At No. 12 Cable Street is the Jack the Ripper Museum (jacktherippermuseum.com).

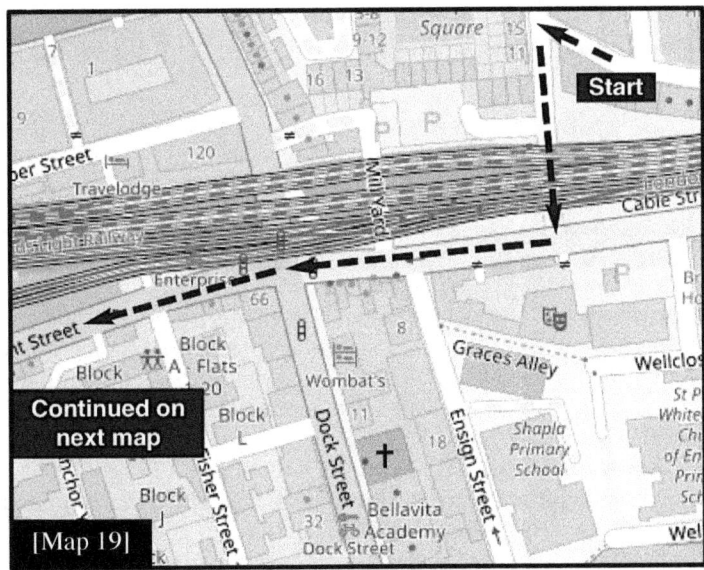

[Map 19]

173

As you cross over the next intersection Cable Street becomes Royal Mint Street. You will note the mix of properties includes former warehouses with a particularly fine example being that which today is The Artful Dodger public house on your left (**soft.loses.surely**) **[87]**. The current building was erected in 1825 and altered in 1881, and again in 1888. The original pub name was the Crown and Seven Stars (referring to The Plough constellation) and was on this site certainly from 1715 when Ned Ward wrote it was a place where nearby 'Frippery-Women stand with Stays, Coats, Suits, and Breeches second hand' and 'Where rags of every sort and size are sold and thieves their daily correspondence hold'. When rebuilt in 1825 the proprietorship passed to a German victualler, Diederich Menke, who opened wine vaults which were advertised in 1829 as being 'recently built, in a most substantial manner, with superior elevation ... spacious lofty liquor shop, warehouse, kitchens, ample cellarage and vaults'.

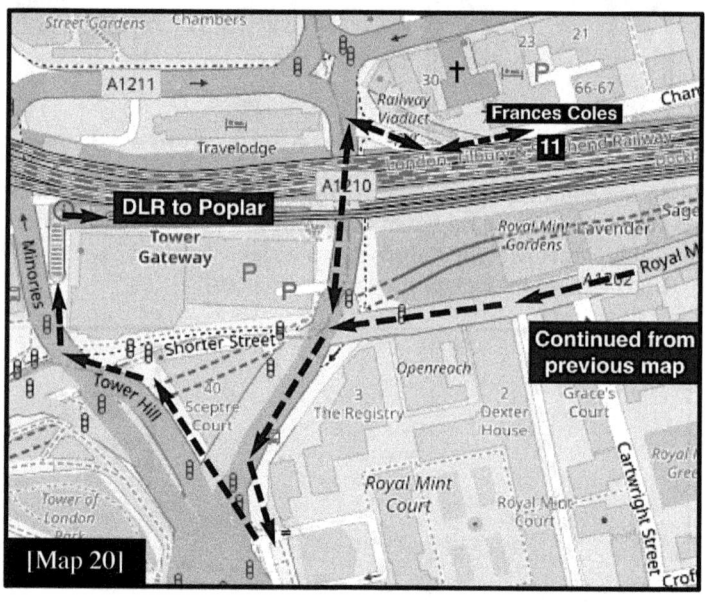

Royal Mint Street **[88]** was where James Sadler was observed to be 'drunk and bloodied' on the night of Frances Coles' murder (**85**). Keep going to the end of Royal Mint Street, and the major junction with Mansell Street. Turn into Mansell Street and go back under the railway line. Immediately after you have done this turn right into Chamber Street. This road will go under another former spur of the London, Tilbury & Southend Railway. As you immerge from under the bridge you will see an iron pillar supporting the railway line. The enclosed unit to the left of the pillar is where Swallow Street once ran through to Royal Mint Street, and where the body of Francis Coles was found (**cheese.cities.cape**) (**83**).

ॐ 12 ॐ
CATHERINE MYLETT, POPLAR HIGH STREET
⇐40 minutes ⇒

Retrace your steps to the junction of Mansell Street and Royal Mint Street. Continue straight following the wall of the old Royal Mint into East Smithfield. A little way along here you will see Tower Bridge in front of you, the Tower of London to your right, and the entrance to the old Royal Mint on your left (**ozone.fend.with**) **[89]**. It was here that James Sadler was found 'drunk and bloodied' by a patrolling officer (**85**). The magnificent building (Royal Mint Court) beyond the gates is a development of offices, retail, and leisure space. As the name suggests this was the site of the Royal Mint from 1809 until 1967, and prior to that was a Cistercian abbey from 1348 until the dissolution of the monasteries when it was taken over by the Royal Navy as a victualling yard, and latterly a tobacco warehouse. The most recent development was announced in 2018 when the site was sold to the People's Republic of China to be used for their new London embassy.

Cross the road at the pedestrian crossing and enter Tower Hill, keeping the Tower of London to your left. Cross over the next road (Shorter Street) and as the road bears right into Minories you will see the escalator which takes you to Tower Gateway station on the Docklands Light Railway (**voices.bands,grace**). Board any train that goes to Poplar (4 stops) – this will include trains that terminate at Beckton or Woolwich Arsenal, but not Lewisham. The journey time is 8 minutes. Alight at Poplar station [**Map 21**] and take the Poplar High Street exit i.e. not the one that goes up stairs, but the one at the far end of the platform that descends to street level. There is a lift if needed.

Follow the pedestrian signs out of the station and toward Poplar High Street. This will take you down the side of New City College and to Poplar High Street itself where you will turn right. It was in this street that Elizabeth Stride ran a coffee shop (**29**). Continue past Hale Street to Woodstock Terrace on your left-hand-side. Note the magnificently restored Lansbury Heritage Hotel on the corner. Turn up Woodstock Terrace and immediately next to the hotel you will see the entrance

Jack the Ripper Walks

to St. Mattias Old Church (**joined.pokers.enter**) (**75**) which has changed little in appearance since it was built by the East India Company in 1654 [**90**]. Today it is the local community centre so is not open to the public.

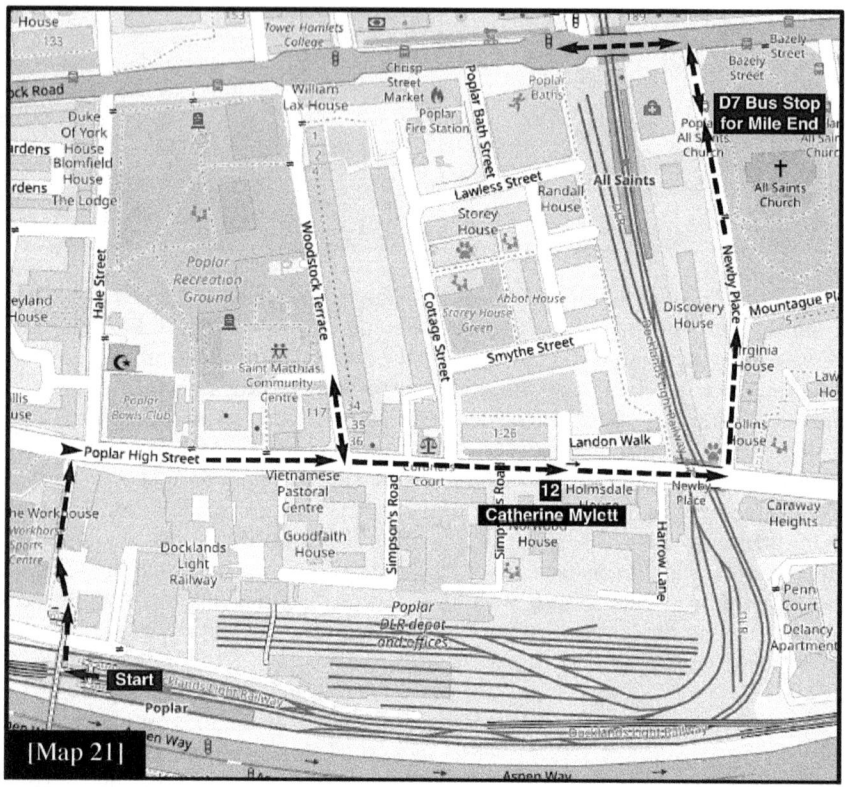

[Map 21]

Retrace your steps back to Poplar High Street turning left to continue along this road. On the corner of Cottage Street (the next left turn) you will see a fine example of an early 20th century purpose-built coroners court (**option.flock.reds**) (**54**). A little further along on your right-hand-side is Holmsdale House. It is close to the ramp that Clarke's Yard was located. This is where the body of Catherine Mylett was discovered on the 20th December 1888 (**goals.gains.struck**) (**73**).

From here continue on over the railway bridge to Newby Place and turn left into this street. At the far end on the right-hand-side is the imposing All Saints Church which was built between 1821-1823 as the parish church of the newly created district of Poplar (**last.glue.cave**)[**91**]. The Ionic columns of the portico are surmounted by a façade of Corinthian columns rising to an elegant steeple 160 feet high. The structure built was just one of 36 plans received, and cost over £33,000 to construct against an initial budget of £20,000. Rectors of the church were supported by the generous patronage of Brasenose College, Oxford.

[90]

[91]

Outside the church is the bus stop (also the terminus) for the D7 bus to Mile End station (the terminus at the other end of this route). You should board a D7 (and go to the top deck if possible) as the bus takes you on a tour of Docklands including the Isle of Dogs, Island Gardens, Masthouse Terrace Pier, Canary Wharf, and Westferry. There is a bus every 4-8 minutes during the day (Monday to Friday) with a journey time of around 45 minutes.

[92]

If you have time go to the top of the road and turn left into East India Dock Road. It was in this road that Elizabeth Stride once had lodgings while running a coffee shop in Poplar High Street (**29**). A little way along, just past All Saints station, is another reminder of a bygone era in the shape of Poplar Baths (**deals.woes.deep**) [**92**]. Much larger the wash houses in Old Castle Street (**79**) these were constructed in 1933 and were operational until 1988. However, there has been a bath house on this site since 1852 providing public washing facilities for the poor. The slipper section contained 12 baths for men (1st class), 24 for men (2nd class), and 6 for women (1st and 2nd class).

There were steam and shower facilities, as well as washing tubs, drying equipment, and ironing rooms. The 1933 building converted one of the baths into a general space for 1,400 persons for use as a dance hall, cinema, exhibition centre, and on occasion a sports hall for boxing and wrestling. Today the restored building is a leisure centre incorporating 100 new homes.

The statue outside is of a local Blackwall man Richard Green (and his dog Hector). He was a shipbuilder of some note, and also a philanthropist. The bas reliefs show 2 of his ships – the *Arapiles* [**93**] which was still under construction at the time of his death in 1863, and the record-breaking tea clipper *Challenger* [**94**].

❧ 13 ❧
ADA WILSON, MAIDMAN STREET
⇐75 minutes ⇒

Alight from the D7 bus at the Mile End station terminus in Grove Road [**Map 22**]. A little further up this road you will see a railway bridge. On the 13th June 1944 the first V-1 rocket to land on London hit the bridge destroying several houses and killing 6 people. You should see several paths going into Mile End Park (**61**). Take any one of these and follow it up and over 'The Green Bridge'. As the path descends the other side you will come to an intersection with 2 paths, both of which have steps going down (that on your right-hand-side leading to a large pond/water feature) (**hobby.school.boring**). This is the approximate location of where Maidman Street ran east to west from Burdett Road to Canal Road parallel to Mile End Road. It was here that the attempted murder of Ada Wilson took place in March 1888 (**58**). Continue on the main path which will curve round as it follows the line of the pond/water feature. It ends at a bridge over the Regent's

Canal (**dozed.prep.poems**). Do not go over the bridge, but turn right and walk back along the towpath keeping the canal to your left. This will take you back to Mile End Road, where you should cross the road. From the other side you will see Mile End Lock in the distance (**wiping.trim.badge**) [95].

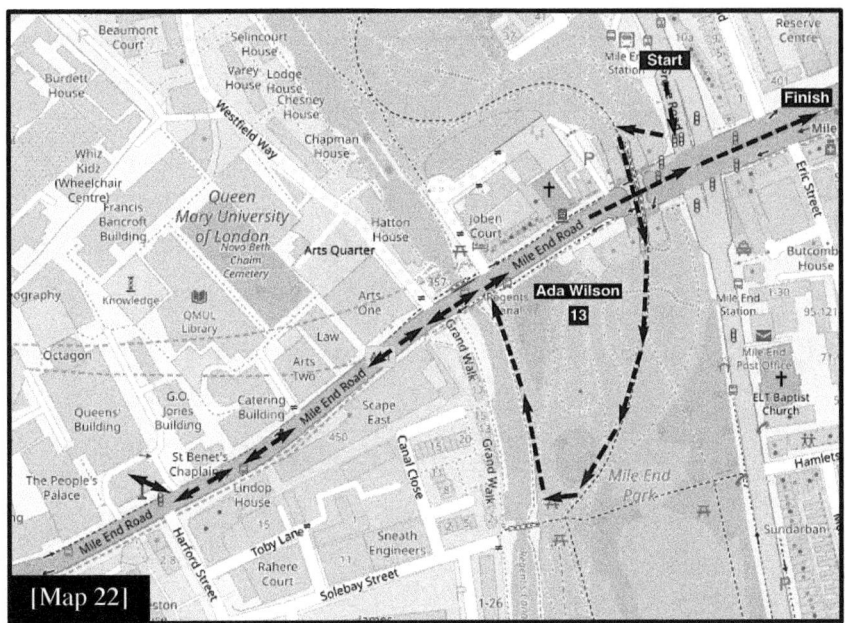

[Map 22]

The Regent's Canal is just under 9 miles in length and runs from Paddington Basin and the Grand Union Canal in the west, to the Limehouse Basin and the River Thames in the east. Work started in 1812 with the Camden to Limehouse section which opened in 1820. With the rise of the railways, in particular the Midland Railway, the canal suffered a long decline from the beginning of the 20th century. In fact, as early as 1845 and 1859, there were schemes to convert the canal to a railway. Today commercial vessels have given way to leisure craft, while the towpath has become the domain of cyclists and pedestrians.

From here you could turn right, go under 'The Green Bridge', across the next intersection, and on to Mile End Underground station where this tour ends. However, if you have time, turn left along Mile End Road to visit some further locations of interest.

The first, on your right-hand-side, looks like it could be an observatory, but is, in fact, St. Benet's Chaplaincy of Queen Mary University of London (**elbow.logic.ruler**) [96]. The current building replaces a former Church of

England mission church (which held 900 worshippers) dating from 1872 that was destroyed by bombing during World War II. It was constructed in 1962, and in 1964 the interior walls of the circular dome were decorated with a series of murals designed by renowned Polish ceramicist, Adam Kossowski, who employed a sgraffito technique.

Just beyond, still on your right-hand-side and also part of the University, is The People's Palace (**healthier.reply.solar**) **[97]**. It is a little confusing since the building that proclaims itself to be The People's Palace should more accurately be called the Great Hall, a fine Grade II listed structure that is used as a theatre and entertainment centre. It was opened on the 13th February 1937 by King George VI, and was his first official engagement as monarch.

The actual People's Palace is the much finer adjacent building known today as the Queen's Building **[98]**. This structure dates from 1887, but was destroyed by fire in 1931 and thought to be beyond repair so the replacement building (the Great

Hall) was constructed next door. Interestingly, as the original was also rebuilt there are now, in effect, 2 People's Palaces on the same site. The original 1887 complex included a large concert hall, library, gymnasium, swimming pool, garden, and tennis court. Much of the funding was from John Beaumont who bequeathed funding in order to promote the education and entertainment of the poor in the area around Beaumont Square. While here note the drinking fountain and clock tower which was 'presented to the trustees of the Peoples' Palace for the benefit of the people of East London by Herbert Stern Esq in memory of his father Baron de Stern' **[99]**.

From here retrace your steps along Mile End Road. Just before 'The Garden Bridge' you will pass the Roman Catholic Church of The Guardian Angels (**joke.talent.riots**) **[100]**. It dates from 1903 and, rather touchingly, was paid for by Henry Fitzalan-Howard, 15th Duke of Norfolk, in memory of his youngest sister, Lady Margaret Howard, who had lived and performed charitable works in the area.

Pass under the bridge, cross the intersection with Burdett Road, and on your right-hand-side you will see Mile End Underground station where this tour ends.

Congratulations – you have now completed *The Grand Tour* of all 13 possible Jack the Ripper sites. From here Central and District line trains run to central London where you will find easy access to all parts of the Capital and beyond.

Acknowledgments

All the photographs in this publication, with the exception of those acknowledged here, are by the author, or already in the public domain (www.commons.wikimedia.org). Particularly useful sources of illustrations include the Associated Newspapers Limited archive, and original publications such as *The Illustrated Police News*, *The Penny Illustrated Paper*, *Funny Folks Magazine*, *London Old & New*, and *Living London*. The Gustave Doré drawings are courtesy of the Wellcome Library, London, and the world map on page 9 is courtesy of The Norman B. Leventhal Map & Educational Center at Boston Public Library. The various 1888 maps are based on those found at www.theundergroundmap.com, while [**Map 1**] to [**Map 22**] utilise www.openstreetmap.org, with physical locations being defined by www.What3Words.com.

References & Further Reading

When it comes to Jack the Ripper there is no shortage of books on the subject. The problem is that many contain factual errors, and are contradictory in nature – and this applies equally to those reports written at the time. It is hoped that this author has avoided the various pitfalls and presents here works that should belong to every 'Ripperologist', those interested in the history of London, and/or its railways.

Jack the Ripper

Begg, Paul, *Jack the Ripper The Definitive History*, 310 pages, Pearson Education Limited, (2003), ISBN: 978-0-582506-31-2.

Clack, Robert & Hutchinson, Philip, *The London of Jack the Ripper Then and Now*, 190 pages, Breedon Books Publishing, (2007), ISBN: 978-1-859836-00-2.

Evans, Stuart P. & Rumbelow, Donald, *Jack the Ripper Scotland Yard Investigates*, 303 pages, Sutton Publishing, (2006), ISBN: 978-0-750942-28-7.

Evans, Stuart P. & Skinner, Keith, *The Ultimate Jack the Ripper Companion*, 758 pages, Carroll & Graf, (2000), ISBN: 978-0-786709-26-7.

Evans, Stuart P. & Skinner, Keith, *Jack the Ripper Letters From Hell*, 306 pages, Sutton Publishing, (2001), ISBN: 978-0-750925-49-5.

Evans, Stuart P. & Skinner, Keith, *Jack the Ripper and the Whitechapel Murders*, 12 pages, Public Record Office, (2002), ISBN: 978-1-903365-39-7.

Fido, Martin, *The Crimes, Detection & Death of Jack the Ripper*, 241 pages, Weidenfeld & Nicolson, ISBN: 978-0-297791-36-2.

Horsler, Val, *Jack the Ripper*, 112 pages, The National Archives, (2007), ISBN: 978-1-905615-14-8.

Rivett, Miriam & Whitehead, Mark, *Jack the Ripper*, 96 pages, Pocket Essentials, (2001), ISBN: 978-1-903047-69-9.

Sugden, Philip, *The Complete History of Jack the Ripper*, 532 pages, Carroll & Graf, (1994), ISBN: 978-0-786709-32-8.

www.casebook.org – an excellent source of information on Jack the Ripper which also has links to the contemporary records.

www.jack-the-ripper.org – another excellent source of information on everything Jack the Ripper.

www.whitechapelsociety.com – website of The Whitechapel Society, a long-established historical society dedicated to studies of Jack the Ripper as well as wider aspects of Victorian and Edwardian east London.

LONDON

Sims, George R., *Living London*, Volumes I-III, Cassell and Company, Limited, (1903).

Weinreb, Ben (Editor) & Hibbert, Christopher (Editor), *The London Encyclopaedia*, 1120 pages, MacMillan Reference, (2010), ISBN: 978-1-405049-25-2.

Walford, Edward, *Old and New London: A narrative of its History, its People, and its Places*, Volumes I-VI, Cassell & Company, Limited, (1902).

RAILWAYS

Dow, George, *London, Tilbury & Southend Album*, 120 pages, Ian Allan, (1981), ISBN: 978-0-711010-85-7.

Nicholls, Geoff & Eccles, Steve, *Fenchurch Street Station*, 29 pages, British Rail Eastern Region Public Affairs Department.

Searle, Muriel V., *Down the Line to Southend*, 196 pages, The Baton Press Limited, (1984), ISBN: 978-0-85936-243-6.

www.railwaysarchive.co.uk – source for original railway accident reports.

GENERAL INDEX

Adventure of the Copper Beeches, The 13
Adventure of the Priory School, The 101
Almshouses 75
Angel of Justice (statue) 124
Angel of Liberty (statue) 124
Angel of Peace (statue) 124
Anorexia nervosa 95
Antimony 121
Arapiles (ship) 178
Arsenic 97
Ashenazy Acquisations 152, 156

Battle of Cable Street, The 172
Bluecoat boys 147, 168
'Bow Bells' 60
Bow Porcelain 60
Bright's Disease 40, 95
British Union of Fascists, The 172
Bury St. Edmunds, Abbot of 148, 167
'Bus Stop Stalker' 122
Bywell Castle 33

'Camden Ripper' The 122
Camden Town Murder, The 98
Catholic (faith) 95
Central Line (Underground) 181
Central News Agency 27
Challenger (ship) 178
Chancery, The 147, 168
Charity Organisations Society 71
Christian (faith) 90, 117, 129, 133, 154, 159, 179
Circle Line (Underground) 107, 117
City of London, The 35, 37, 38, 40, 47, 65, 90, 104, 107, 113, 115, 116, 119, 141, 144, 145, 148, 152, 156, 166, 168, 169, 170, 171
City of London boundary marker 65, 90, 144, 170
City of London Cemetery (Manor Park) 40
City of London police 38, 40
Clinical Society 95
Co-operative Wholesale Society 142, 170
Coldstream Guards 68

185

Coroner's Court 54-55
Corporation of the City of London 40, 118, 152, 156
'Crazy Gang', The 131, 155
Criminal Investigation Department (CID) 40, 41
Cutlers, Worshipful Company of 148, 166
Czarist 98

'Dear Boss' letters 26, 27, 39, 92
Depression, The Long 13
Diary of Jack the Ripper, The 97
District Line (Underground) 106, 181
DNA evidence 96, 99

East End Dwelling Company, The 43
East London Observer 24
East London Railway 106
Edict of Nantes 53

Famous Crimes Past and Present 66
Fez (ship) 85
Four Per Cent Industrial Dwelling Company Ltd. 43, 138, 161
Freemasonry 95, 96
From Hell (film) 133, 159
'From Hell' (letter) 40
Fullerian Professor of Physiology 95
Funny Folks Magazine 183

Goulston Street Graffito, The 38, 39, 41, 89-90, 94, 109, 149, 165
Great Eastern Railway 106
Great Russian Criminals 98
Greater London Council 126
Grenadier Guards 67
Guild of Artillery 52
Guinness Trust, The 43
Hammersmith Nude Murders, The 121
Headless Criminal Investigation Department, The 40
Home Office, The 27, 89, 90
Hop-picking/Hopping 34, 42
Houndsditch Murders 148, 166
Huguenots 53, 129, 133, 134, 154, 159, 160

Illustrated Police News, The 15, 21, 22, 29, 34, 41, 44, 59, 62, 65, 73, 76, 83, 84, 183

Indexes

Improved Industrial Dwelling Company 43

Jack the Ripper: The Final Solution 96, 99, 100
Jack the Ripper's Bedroom 98
'Jack the Stripper' 121
Jewish (faith) 13, 26, 38, 39, 43, 47, 53, 76, 89, 90, 92, 94, 96, 101, 102, 103, 124, 126, 139, 142, 145, 147, 148, 167, 169, 171
Joi (alternative dub/dance music DJ team) 134, 160

Knighten Guild 145, 168

'Lambeth Poisoner', The 121
'Leather Apron' 26, 27, 91, 102
Liberty Bell, The 21
'Lipski' 32, 89, 92
Living London 183
London & Blackwall Railway 80, 82, 86
London: A Pilgrimage 10
London, Brighton & South Coast Railway 106
London, Chatham & Dover Railway 106
London County Council 43
London Old & New 183
London, Tilbury & Southend Railway 82, 86, 171, 174
London, University of 21, 179, 180
Lord Mayor's Show, The 47, 104, 118

'Match girls', The 60, 130, 155
Methodist (faith) 129, 154
Metropolitan Board of Works 69
Metropolitan Drinking Fountain (and Cattle Trough) Association 146, 168
Metropolitan Line (Underground) 117, 145, 168
Midland Railway 179
Model Dwellings 38, 39, 42, 43, 69, 131, 138, 149, 155, 161, 165
Murder by Decree (film) 100
Mystery of Jack the Ripper, The 99
Myxoedema 95

Navigating the Dark (series of artworks) 152, 156

Octavia Hill (dwelling company) 43
Oliver Twist 118, 119
Olympic Games, London 2012 61
Osborn Street Murder, The 64

Over London by Rail 9

Paraplegia 95
Parliamentary voting list 54
Peabody Donation Fund/Peabody Trust 43, 131, 155
Peabody Trust – See Peabody Donation Fund
Penny Illustrated Paper, The 34, 84, 183
Pinchin Street Torso, The 78, 80-82, 171, 173
Populus canescens 75
Populus nigra 75
Portrait of a Killer: Jack the Ripper – Case Closed 99
Princess Alice/Princess Alice disaster 30, 33

Quaker (faith) 59

Rainham Mystery, The 81
Renatus Harris organ 146, 168
Robinson Crusoe 146, 168
Royal family, The 95, 99, 100
Royal Navy 175
Russian government 98
Russian secret police 98

Salvation Army, The 28
'Saucy Jack' postcard 39, 40
Scotland Yard 27, 48, 81, 86
Scotland Yard Central Office 48
Seaman's Union 86
South Eastern Railway 106
Spitalfields in ye Olden Time – visiting a Weaver's Shop 133, 159
'Stockwell Strangler', The 122
Strychnine 94, 121
Study in Scarlet, A 8, 119
Sulphuric acid 121

'Teacup Poisoner', The 121
Thames Conservancy Board 33
Thames Torso Murders, The 81
Tottenham & Hampstead Junction Railway 114

Unicorn, The 163
United Grand Lodge of England 96

V-1 rocket 178

Wash Houses 79, 165, 177
Wellington Barracks 68
Whitechapel & Bow Railway 106
Whitechapel Division (Metropolitan Police) 51, 102
Whitechapel Murders/Horrors/Mystery 7-13, 26, 27, 51, 57, 62, 81
Whitechapel Society, The 184
Whitechapel Vigilance Committee 28, 40
Why Detectives Don't Detect 41
'Wolfman', The 122
Women's Social Work 28
Wooden Boat with Seven People (sculpture) 152, 156
Working Lad's Institute (Whitechapel) 25, 125

Yves Saint Laurent (shop) 122

PERSONS INDEX

Abberline, Frederick (Detective Inspector) 48, 132, 133, 156, 159
Albrook, Lizzie 45
Allen, Chesney 131, 155
Anderson, Dr. Sir Robert (Assistant Police Commissioner) 41, 48, 74, 78, 96, 102, 103
Andrews, Walter (Police Constable) 77
Arnold, Thomas (Police Superintendent) 39
Atlee, Clement 70

Barnaby (dog) 40, 41, 48
Barnardo, Dr. Thomas John 21, 47, 90
Barnett, Joseph 45, 51, 93-94, 116, 119
Barrett, Thomas (Police Constable) 67, 68
Baxter, Wynne 75
Beaumont, John 181
Bellfield, Levi 122
Benjiman, Corporal 68
Beveridge, William 70
Bierman, Rose 58
'Black' Mary – See Kelly, Mary
Blizard, Sir William 21

189

Bond, Dr. Thomas 37, 48, 49, 50, 74, 75, 77, 90, 91
Booth Charles 28
Booth, William 28
Boswell, James 7
Bowyer, Thomas 47
Brown, Frederick 36
Brownfield, Dr. Matthew 74, 75
Bryant, Alice – See McKenzie, Alice
Burdett-Coutts, Angela 63
Burgho (dog) 40, 41, 48

Cadosch, Albert 24
Callana, Ellen 85
Campbell, Donald 85
Cass, Sir John 147, 168
Chapman, Annie (Annie Siffey, Annie Sivvy, 'Dark Annie') 21-28, 33, 91, 94, 104, 108, 123, 125, 127, 128, 154
Chapman, John 22
'Cheese cutter hat' (suspect) 85, 86
Christie, John 121
'Clay Pipe' Alice – See McKenzie, Alice
Cohen, Aaron Davis (Davis Cohen, Nathan Kaminsky) 96
Cohen, Davis – See Cohen, Aaron Davis
Cole, Frances – See Coles, Frances
Coles, Frances (Frances Cole) 48, 77, 83-86, 137, 161, 173, 174
Coles, James 84
Coles, Mary 84
Connelly, Mary ('Pearly Poll') 67, 68
Conway, Catherine – See Eddowes, Catherine
Conway, Thomas 34
Cornwell, Patricia 99
Cox, Mary 45, 46
Cream, Dr. Thomas Neill 94, 121
Cross, Charles 15, 126
Crow, Alfred 65
Culpeper, Nicholas, 132

'Dark Annie' – See Chapman, Annie
'Dark' Mary – See Kelly, Mary
Davies/Davis (husband of Mary Kelly) 44
Davis (husband of Catherine Mylett) 73
Davis/Davies (husband of Mary Kelly) 44
Davis, Abraham 136, 159

Davis, Florence 73
Davis, John 24
Defoe, Daniel 52, 146, 168
Dickens, Charles 116, 118, 130, 154
Diemschutz, Louis 32
Dimmock, Emily 98
Dixon, George 76
Donovan, Timothy 22
Doré, Gustave 9, 10, 138, 145, 161, 164, 169, 149, 183
Dowler, Milly 122
Doyle, Sir Arthur Conan 41
Druitt, Montague 95, 97
'Drunken Lizzie' Davis – See Mylett, Catherine
Duke of Clarence and Avondale – See Victor, Prince Albert Christian Edward

Eddowes, Catherine (Catherine Kelly, Catherine Conway) 34-41, 48, 78, 89, 90, 91, 96, 116, 123, 136, 138, 139, 143, 147, 153, 154, 156, 159, 161, 165, 167, 168
Eddy, Prince – See Victor, Prince Albert Christian Edward
Elliott, George (Police Constable) 83
Erskine, Kenneth 122

'Fair Alice' Downey – See Mylett, Catherine
'Fair' Emma – See Kelly, Mary
Fitzalan-Howard, Henry (15th Duke of Norfolk) 181
Flanagan, Bud 28, 131, 155
Flanagan, James (Detective Inspector) 84
Fossan, Lewis 135, 159
Fossan, Thomas 135, 158
Foster, Elizabeth 45, 133, 159
Fournier, George 53, 134, 160

George (Private) 68
George V, King 20
George VI, King 180
'Ginger' – See Kelly, Mary
Golding, Robert (Police Sergeant) 73
Goodman, Roland 142, 170
Graham, Rodney 163
Green, Richard 178
Gull, Sir William Withey 95-96, 99
Gustafsdotter, Elizabeth – See Stride, Elizabeth

Hague, Mrs. (landlady) 84
Haigh, John 121
Hames, Margaret (Margaret Hayes) 64
Hardy, Anthony 122
Harvey, Maria 45
Hawksmoor, Nicholas 133, 159
Hayes, Margaret – See Hames, Margaret
Hector (dog) 178
Henry I, King 60
Henry VIII, King 75
Hinton (Police Constable) 83
Holland, Emily 18, 19, 139, 163
Holmes, Sherlock 13, 41, 93, 89, 101, 119
Howard, Lady Margaret 181
Hutchinson, George 47, 51, 138, 161
Hyde, Frederick (Police Constable) 83

Ireland. Mungo 121
Isenschmidt, Jacob 26

Jackson, Elizabeth 81
Jerrold, Blanchard 10
Johnson, Dr. Samuel 7
Jones, Sir Horace 35

Kaminsky, Nathan – See Cohen, Aaron Davis
Kelly, Catherine – See Eddowes, Catherine
Kelly, John 34
Kelly, Marie Jeanette – See Kelly, Mary
Kelly, Mary (Marie Jeanette Kelly, 'Fair' Emma, 'Ginger', 'Dark' Mary, 'Black' Mary) 37, 44-51, 62, 66, 73, 77, 78, 84, 91, 92, 93, 94, 99, 100, 104, 111, 123, 132, 133, 135, 137, 138, 147, 151, 152, 154, 157, 159, 160, 161
Kelly, Mary Ann – see Eddowes, Catherine 35
Kidney, Michael 30
Killeen, Dr. Timothy 67
Knight, Stephen 96, 99, 100
Konovalov, Vassily (Count Andrey Luiskovo) 98
Kosminski, Aaron 96-97
Kossowski, Adam 180

Lemos, Kalliopi 152, 156
Lester, Thomas 21
Lewis, Sarah 46, 47

Llewellyn, Rees 17
Long, Alfred (Police Constable) 38
Long, Elizabeth 24
'Long Liz' – See Stride, Elizabeth
Luiskovo, Count Andrey – See Konovalov, Vassily
Lupo, Michele de Marco 122
Lusk, George 40

Mackie, Hamish 142, 170
Macnaghten, Sir Melville (Assistant Chief Constable) 81, 95, 96, 97
Maddocks, Thomas 21
Mainwaring, Boulton 21
Mallon, Dr. Jimmy 165
Marr, Timothy 104
Maslen, Thomas 117
Matters, Leonard 99
Maybrick, James 97
McCarthy, John 47
McCormack, John 76
McKenna, Edward 26
McKenzie, Alice (Alice Bryant, 'Clay Pipe' Alice) 37, 48, 62, 66, 74, 76-78, 81, 84, 97, 138, 161, 164, 165
Mellett, Catherine – See Mylett, Catherine
Menke, Diederich 174
Millett, Catherine – See Mylett, Catherine
Millwood, Annie 57-58, 59, 157
Millwood, Richard 57
Mizen, Jonas (Police Constable) 16, 17, 126
Monro, James 51, 81
Montagu, Samuel 28
Mosley, Oswald 172
Mylett, Catherine (Rose Mylett, Catherine Millett, Catherine Mellett, 'Drunken Lizzie' Davis, 'Fair Alice' Downey) 37, 48, 73-75, 77, 78, 175, 176
Mylett, Rose – See Mylett, Catherine

Neil, John (Police Constable) 15, 16, 17
Netley, John 95
Nichols, Mary Ann 'Polly' 15-19, 22, 25, 26, 48, 91, 104, 106, 123, 125, 126, 137, 138, 139, 154, 161, 162, 163
Nichols, William 18
Nilsen, Dennis 121-122

Ostrog, Michael 97-98

Oxley, Dr. Frederick 83

Passmore, George 134, 160
Paul, Robert 15, 126
Peabody, George 43
'Pearly Poll' – See Connelly, Mary
Pedachenko, Dr. Alexander 98
Pennett, William (Police Constable) 80
Phillips, Annie 34
Phillips, Dr. George Bagster 48, 77, 84, 91
Piggott, William 26
Piser, John (John Pizer) 26
Pizer, John – See Piser, John
Prater, Elizabeth 46
Prince Eddy – See Victor, Prince Albert Christian Edward
Proesch, Gilbert 134, 160
Puckeridge, Oswald 26

Rasputin 98
Reid, Edmund (Police Inspector) 47, 62, 65, 68, 77
Richardson, John 23, 26
Robinson, Louis (Police Constable) 34, 143, 168
Rosenberg, Isaac 163
Rothschild, Charles 124
Rothschild, Lady Charlotte 126
Russell, Mary 64
Ryder, Elizabeth 76

Sadler, James 84, 85, 86, 138, 142, 161, 170, 174, 175
Salisbury, Lord 96
Saunders, Dr. William 37, 90
Schmidt, Philip 171
Schumacher, Friedrich 26
Schwartz, Israel 32, 92
Shamsher, Farook 134, 160
Shamsher, Haroon 134, 160
Shepherd family 58
Siffey, Annie – See Chapman, Annie
Sivvy, Annie – See Chapman, Annie
Skipper (Private) 68
Smith, Emma Elizabeth 48, 62-64, 65, 77, 124, 135, 158, 160, 162
Smith, William 32
Soper, Florence 28

Stamp, Sir Samuel 147, 168
Stanley, Dr. 99
Stanley, Herbert 99
Stern, Baron de 181
Stern, Herbert 181
Stride, Elizabeth (Elizabeth Gustafsdotter, 'Long Liz') 29-33, 34, 38, 44, 89, 91, 92, 108, 116, 123, 129, 138, 139, 150, 154, 158, 161, 167, 171, 175, 177
Stride, John 29, 30
Sunley, Bernard 71
Swanson, Donald (Chief Inspector) 25, 33

Tabram, Charles 67
Tabram, Frederick 67
Tabram, Henry 67
Tabram, Martha (Martha Turner) 41, 48, 58, 62, 65-69, 77, 162, 164
Tanner, Elizabeth 30
Thain, John (Police Constable) 17, 18
Thompson, Ernest (Police Constable) 83
Tilly, John 58
Tilly, Nathaniel 58
Toynbee, Arnold 70
Tumblety, Dr. Frances 99-100
Turner, Henry 68
Turner, Martha – See Tabram, Martha

Victor, Prince Albert Christian Edward (Duke of Clarence and Avondale, Prince Eddy) 100
Victoria, Queen 7, 41, 51, 100

Ward, Ned 174
Warren, Sir Charles 25, 27, 38, 41, 43, 51, 78, 89, 90, 94, 96, 98
Watkins, Edward (Police Constable) 35, 147, 167
Watson, Dr. John 8, 13
Wilson, Ada 58-59, 178
Winberg, Levitski 98

Young, Graham 121

PLACES INDEX

Abergeldie 100
Aldgate 109, 143, 145, 168, 170
Aldgate station 109, 110, 111, 116, 145, 168
Aldgate East station 72, 106, 107
All Saints 176
All Saints station 177
Alma public house 24, 127
Altab Ali Park (St. Mary's Park) 139
America, United States of/American 21, 26, 43, 59, 94, 97, 99, 142, 170
Anglican Christ Church 129, 154
Annexe Market – See Smithfield Market
Artful Dodger public house, The 174
Artichoke Inn 21

Balliol House 70, 71
Bangladesh/Bengal/Bengali 43, 65
Barbican station 117
Barking station 113
Battersea Park 81
Beckton 175
Bedfordshire 136, 160
Bermondsey 34, 84
Bermondsey workhouse 84
Bernard Sunley House 71
Bernhard Baron House 139, 171
Bevis Marks Synagogue 147, 167
Big Ben 21, 142, 170
Billingsgate (Fish) Market 45, 93, 116
Birmingham 7, 34
Bishopsgate 52, 153, 156
Bishopsgate police station 34, 35, 91, 109, 132, 136, 142, 153, 156, 159, 170
Bishopsgate station 108
Black Eagle Brewery – See Truman Brewery
Blackheath 95
Blackwall 75, 86, 178
Bow 56, 58, 60-61, 130, 155
Bow Bridge 60
Brady Arts and Community Centre 126
Brady Boys Club 126
Brady Girls Club and Settlement 126

Brasenose College (Oxford) 177
Broadmoor Hospital 122
Broad Street station 114, 118
Broadway (flats) 71, 164
Bristol 7, 163
Bromley 30
Bryant and May (match factory) 60, 130, 155
Buckingham Palace 68
Buck's Row Board School (Trinity Hall) 16, 106, 126
Buenos Aires 99
Burics Marks 148, 167

Camden 98, 179
Canada 94, 99
Canary Wharf 177
Canon Barnett Primary School 164
Charles Booth House 71
Charles Kinloch & Co. Limited 140, 171
Chelsea 45, 81
Chicksand Estate 126, 136
China, People's Republic of (embassy) 175
Christ Church School Spitalfields 134, 160
Christ Church Spitalfields 52, 133, 151, 152, 156, 159, 160
City of London Cemetery (Manor Park) 40
City of London Police 38, 40
Clarke's Yard 73, 74, 176
Coal Exchange, The 90
Commercial Road goods yard 108, 109, 116, 140, 171, 172
Commercial Street police station 132, 142, 156, 170
Co-operative Wholesale Society 142, 170
Crown and Seven Stars public house 174

Deal Street board school (Montefiore Centre) 127
Dutfield's Yard 29, 30, 139, 171

Eastern Dispensary, The 143, 170
East Greenwich 67
East India Docks 75
East London Cemetery 33, 81
Edward VII Memorial, King 124
Eight Bells public house (Ten Bells public House) 45, 132, 133, 134, 151, 159, 160
Essex 60, 114

Essex Wharf 15

Farringdon 106
Fenchurch Street station 82, 86, 113, 114, 118
Finsbury Park 62
Fitzrovia 45
Forest Gate 19, 25
France/French 45, 53, 97, 99, 129, 133, 154, 159
Frying Pan public house 18, 137, 150, 158, 161

Gallions Reach 33
Garrick Theatre 142, 170
George Tavern 73, 74
George Yard Buildings 65, 67, 68, 69, 70, 71, 162, 164
Germany/German 13, 35, 75, 82, 129, 141, 142, 143, 154, 170, 171, 174
German Lutheran Church/Chapel 129, 141, 154, 170, 171
Goodman's Fields 109
Goodman's Fields Horses (sculpture) 142, 170
Gospel Oak 113, 115, 118, 119
Gospel Oak station 114
Goulston Street Model Dwellings (Wentworth Dwellings) 38, 39, 43, 149, 165
Grand Union Canal 179
Great Hall (People's Palace, Queen's Building) 180, 181
Greece/Greek 152, 156
'Green Bridge', The 178, 179
Grosmont 100
Guardian Angels Roman Catholic Church 61, 181
Guy's Hospital 95

Hadland Laboratories 121
Hampstead 113
Hanbury Hall 129, 154
Hanbury House 127
Harry Gosling Primary School 29, 139, 171
Haydon Square goods yard 86, 109, 116
Herbert House 79
Hertfordshire 60
Holmsdale House 176
Hoop and Grapes public house 144, 145, 169
Horn of Plenty public house 45
Hyde Park 40

India/Indian 99, 137, 161

Indexes

Inner Temple (London) 95
International Working Men's Educational Club (IWMEC) 29, 32
Ireland/Irish 44, 45, 99
Island Gardens 177
Isle of Dogs 177
Italy/Italian 143, 170

Jack the Chipper (take away) 138, 162
Jack the Ripper Museum, The 173
Jewish Boy' Club 126
Jew's Temporary Shelter 142, 170
John Cass's Foundation Primary School, Sir 147, 167

Kensington 122
Kent 34, 42
King and Sons (Builders) 79
Kingsland 84
Kingston upon Thames 68

Laindon 113, 115, 119
Laindon station 113, 114, 118
Lambeth Workhouse 18
Lansbury Heritage Hotel 175
La Patente Church 129, 154
Lea, River 60
Leadenhall Market 35
Leman Street police station 85, 132, 142, 156, 170
Lewisham 175
Leytonstone 50
Lilian Knowles House 152, 156
Limehouse 62, 179
Limehouse Basin 179
Limerick 44
Liverpool 7, 97, 99
Liverpool Street station 106, 107, 108, 111, 113, 116, 123, 145, 153, 156, 169
London Central Meat Market – See Smithfield Market
London Fruit Exchange – See London Fruit & Wool Exchange
London Hospital, The (Royal) 20, 21, 56, 64, 124
London Metropolitan University's Women's Library 79
Loughborough Junction 113

Manchester 7, 142, 170
Manor Park 40

Manor Park Cemetery 19, 25
Mansion House station 106
Mark Lane station 107
Masthouse Terrace Pier 177
Merchant House 43
Mile End 154
Mile End Lock 179
Mile End Park 61, 178
Mile End station 61, 154, 177, 178, 179, 181
Miller's Court 44, 45, 47, 46, 52, 111, 147, 151, 154, 157, 159
Minories depot 86
Minories station 86
Montefiore Centre (Deal Street board school) 127
Moorfields 21
Moorgate Street station 113, 114, 117
Moscow 98

Neasden 121
Netherlands/Dutch 42, 79
Newcastle 7
New City College 175
New College (Oxford) 95
New Court 69
New Holland Estate 79
New Scotland Yard 81
North Woolwich station 113
Norwood Junction 113

Old Castle Street Board School 79
Old Ford 60
Oxford 95, 177

Paddington Basin 179
Pakistan/Pakistani 65
Passmore Edwards library 163, 164
Peabody Buildings 53
People's Palace (Queen's Building, Great Hall) 180, 181
Petrograd 98
Petticoat Lane Market 53, 149, 166
Pitsea station 113
Plaistow 33, 82
Poland/Polish 13, 26, 82, 96, 180
Poplar 72, 75, 113, 154, 175, 176

Poplar Baths 177
Poplar Coroner's Court 54
Poplar Fields 75
Poplar New Town 75
Poplar station 175
Poplar workhouse 29
Princess Alice public house 85
Priory of the Holy Trinity 146, 168
Portugal/Portuguese 148, 167
Providence Row night refuge 12, 153, 156

Queen Mary University of London 179, 180
Queen's Building (Queen Mary University of London) 180
Queen's Head public house 30, 151, 158

Regent's Canal 178, 179
Regent's Park 40
Rothschild Buildings 138, 161
Royal Cambridge Music Hall 76
Royal College of Surgeons, The 21
Royal Institution of Great Britain, The 95
Royal Mint, The 85, 175
Royal Mint Court 175
Russia/Russian 13, 82, 97, 98

St. Benet's Chaplaincy (Queen Mary University of London) 179
St. Botolph's (church) 145, 168
St. George Brewery 135
St. George's German Lutheran Church 142, 170
St. Georges-in-the-East 82
St. Jude's (church) 164
St. Mary-le-Bow (church) 60
St. Mary Matfelon (church) 139
St. Mary's Bow (church)
St. Mary's Park – See Altab Ali Park
St. Mary Spital (church) 52
St. Mary's station 106
St. Mattias Old Church 75, 176
St. Patrick's Roman Catholic Cemetery 50
Sandringham 100
Scotland 100
Second Home (Hanbury Street) 128
Sheerness 33

Shoreditch 48
Shoreditch station 108
Shoreditch Town Hall 49
Smithfield 117
Smithfield Market (Annexe Market, London Central Meat Market, West Smithfield Market) 35, 116, 117, 118, 119, 145, 169
Smithfield Park 117
Southend-on-Sea 86, 113, 142, 171
South Grove Workhouse 57
Spain/Spanish 148, 167
Spitalfields 11, 28, 43, 44, 45, 52, 53, 57, 62, 128, 133, 159
Spitalfields Chambers 57, 85, 157
Spitalfields Coal Depot 107
Spitalfields Fruit & Wool Exchange 46, 52, 53, 151, 152, 157
Spitalfields Market 52, 53, 132, 152, 156, 157, 160
Stepney 45, 86
Stepney Green station 106
Still and Star public house 145, 169
Stoke Newington 113
Stratford 60, 61
Sugar House 142, 143, 170

Taylor's cocoa factory 64, 162
Ten Bells public house (Eight Bells public house) 45, 132, 133, 134, 151, 159, 160
Tenter Ground Estate 58
Thames, River 33, 34, 81, 121, 179
Thames Tunnel 107
Tilbury 86, 113, 114
Tower Bridge 35, 175
Tower Gateway station 87, 175
Tower of London, The 68, 144, 169, 175
Toynbee Hall 69-71, 165
Trafalgar Square 51
Trinity Hall (Buck's Row Board School) 16, 106, 126
Tripcock Point 33
Truman Brewery (Black Eagle Brewery) 24, 28, 53, 65, 128
Turkey/Turkish 152, 156

United Free Methodists Church 129, 154

Victoria Park 63

Wadham House 70
Wales/Welsh 44
Wapping station 106
Wellington Barracks 68
Wentworth Dwellings – See Goulston Street Model Dwellings
West Horndon station 114
West India Docks 75
Westferry 177
West London and Liberal Jewish Synagogue 139, 171
Westminster 74
Westminster Abbey 20, 21
West Smithfield Market – See Smithfield Market
Wheeler Estate 58
Whitechapel 9, 11, 12, 22, 25, 28, 38, 48, 51, 52, 56, 62, 91, 96, 99, 102, 103, 104, 113, 114, 115, 119, 126, 128, 139
Whitechapel Art Gallery/Whitechapel Gallery 163, 164
Whitechapel Bell Foundry, The 20, 21, 148, 166
Whitechapel Library 164
Whitechapel (Mile End) station 15, 105, 106, 107, 108, 123, 124, 125, 154
Whitechapel Road 18, 19, 20, 21, 33, 104, 124, 125
Whitechapel Wash House 79, 165
Whitechapel Workhouse Infirmary 57
Woolwich Arsenal 175
Working Lad's Institute (Whitechapel) 25, 125

York 100
Yorkshire 100

STREETS INDEX

Aaron Alley – See Castle Alley
Adler Street 139
Aldgate High Street 34, 104, 109, 143, 144, 145, 167, 168, 169
Aldgate Square 167
Alie Street 142, 143, 170
Angel Court 67
Artillery Lane 52, 53, 153, 156
Artillery Passage 153, 156

Back Church Lane 82, 139, 171, 173

203

Beaumont Square 181
Bell Lane 52
Berner Street (Henriques Street) 29, 30, 32, 92, 139
Bevis Marks 147, 167
Bishopsgate 52, 153, 156
'Blood Alley' (Harrow Alley) 145, 169
Blue Boar Alley 110
Bow Road 113
Brady Street 125
Brick Lane 18, 24, 28, 45, 52, 53, 63, 64, 65, 77, 128, 134, 135, 136, 138, 158, 160, 161, 162
Brompton Road 122
Browne's Lane 28
Brushfield Street 151, 152, 156, 157
Buck's Row (Durward Street) 15, 16, 17, 107, 123, 125, 126
Burdett Road 61, 63, 178, 181

Cable Street 172, 173, 174
Canal Road 61, 178
Castle Alley (Aaron Alley, Castle Court, Moses Alley) 77, 78-79, 164
Castle Court – See Castle Alley
Castle Street 78
Chamber Street 83, 86, 87, 174
Cheapside 60
Chelsea Embankment 81
Chicksand Street 160
Christian Street 82, 171, 172
Church Passage 35, 147, 167
Commercial Road 66, 70, 72, 73, 75, 82, 104, 108, 135, 139, 160
Commercial Street 28, 43, 45, 53, 58, 85, 104, 131, 132, 133, 134, 136, 137, 149, 151, 155, 156, 158, 159, 160, 161, 164, 165
Cottage Street 176
Court Street 124
Cranley Gardens 121
Crispin Street 12, 52, 58, 142, 151, 156, 159
Cutler Street 148, 149, 166

Devonshire Square 166
Devonshire Street 30
Dorset Street 22, 44, 45, 48, 151, 152, 157, 159
Dukes Place 147, 167
Durward Street (Buck's Row) 15, 16, 17, 107, 123, 125, 126

Indexes

East India Dock Road 29, 72, 75, 177
East Smithfield 175

Fairclough Street 139, 171
Farrance Street 63
Fashion Street (Fossan Street) 35, 53, 135, 136, 151, 158, 159, 160
Fleur de Lis Street 132, 155
Flower and Dean Street 29, 30, 31, 34, 35, 47, 77, 111, 135, 136, 138, 150, 158, 160, 161
Flower and Dean Walk 138, 161
Folgate Street, 131, 155, 156
Fort Street 53
Fossan Street (Fashion Street) 35, 53, 135, 136, 151, 158, 159, 160
Fournier Street 45, 53, 132, 134, 160

George Street (Casson Street) 135, 160
George Street (Lolesworth Street) 62, 135, 138, 160, 161
George Street (near St. George Brewery) 45, 135, 160
George Yard 65, 67, 69, 71
Goring Street 148, 167
Goulston Street 38, 39, 70, 78, 89, 90, 116, 149, 165
Greatorex Street 127
Grove Road 178
Gun Street 53, 76
Gunthorpe Street 69, 71, 164

Hale Street 175
Hanbury Street 16, 21, 23, 24, 25, 26, 28, 94, 108, 125, 126, 127, 128, 129, 131, 132, 154, 155
Harrow Alley ('Blood Alley') 145, 169
Harrow Place 149, 166
Henriques Street (Berner Street) 29, 30, 32, 92, 139
Hooper Street 140, 141, 171
Houndsditch 21, 148, 166

John Street 23

Leman Street 85, 86, 140, 142, 170
Little Paternoster Row 45, 152, 157
Little Somerset Street 145, 169
Lolesworth Close 158
Lolesworth Street 31, 135, 138, 150, 160, 161
London Square 71

Lower Thames Street 90

Maidman/Maidmans Street 58, 61, 178
Mansell Street 86, 143, 170, 174, 175
Melrose Avenue 121
Middlesex Street 149, 153, 156, 165, 166
Mile End Road 56, 61, 178, 179, 181
Minories 84, 85, 175
Mitre Square 35, 36, 41, 109, 139, 147, 165, 167
Mitre Street 147, 167
Montague Street/Old Montague Street (Whitechapel) 28, 84, 126
Montagu Street (Marylebone) 25
Moses Alley – See Castle Alley

Newby Place 176
New Court 69
New Fashion Street 58
New Goulston Street 149, 165
Nottingham Street 85

Old Castle Street 79, 165, 177
Old Montague Street – See Montague Street (Whitechapel)
Osborn Street 18, 19, 63, 64, 138, 162

Petticoat Lane 149, 165
Piazza walk 142, 170
Pinchin Street (Rope Walk) 80, 81, 82, 171, 172, 173
Poplar High Street 29, 73, 74, 75, 175, 176, 177
Prince's Road 18

Ratcliffe Highway 45, 104
Resolution Plaza 165
Rillington Place 121
Rope Walk – See Pinchin Street
Rosemary Lane 86
Royal Mint Court 175
Royal Mint Street 83, 86, 87, 174, 175

St. James's Passage – See Church Passage
St. Paul's Road 98
Shepherd's Place 58
Shoreditch High Street 156
Shorter Street 175

Spelman Street 127
Spital Square 156
Star Place 66
Swallow Gardens 83, 86, 87, 173
Swallow Street 84, 87, 174

Thrawl Street 18, 45, 47, 84, 85, 111, 135, 136, 137, 138, 150, 158, 160, 161
Tower Hill 175

Upper North Street 29

Vallance Road 28, 126

Warwick Lane 148, 166
Wentworth Street 9, 43, 69, 70, 135, 138, 149, 160, 161, 162, 164
Whitechapel High Street 77, 78, 79, 104, 138, 162, 165
Whitechapel Road 18, 19, 20, 21, 33, 104, 124, 125
White's Row 57, 58
Widegate Street 153, 156
Wilkes Street 131, 155
Woodstock Terrace 175

If you enjoyed this publication you may also like ...

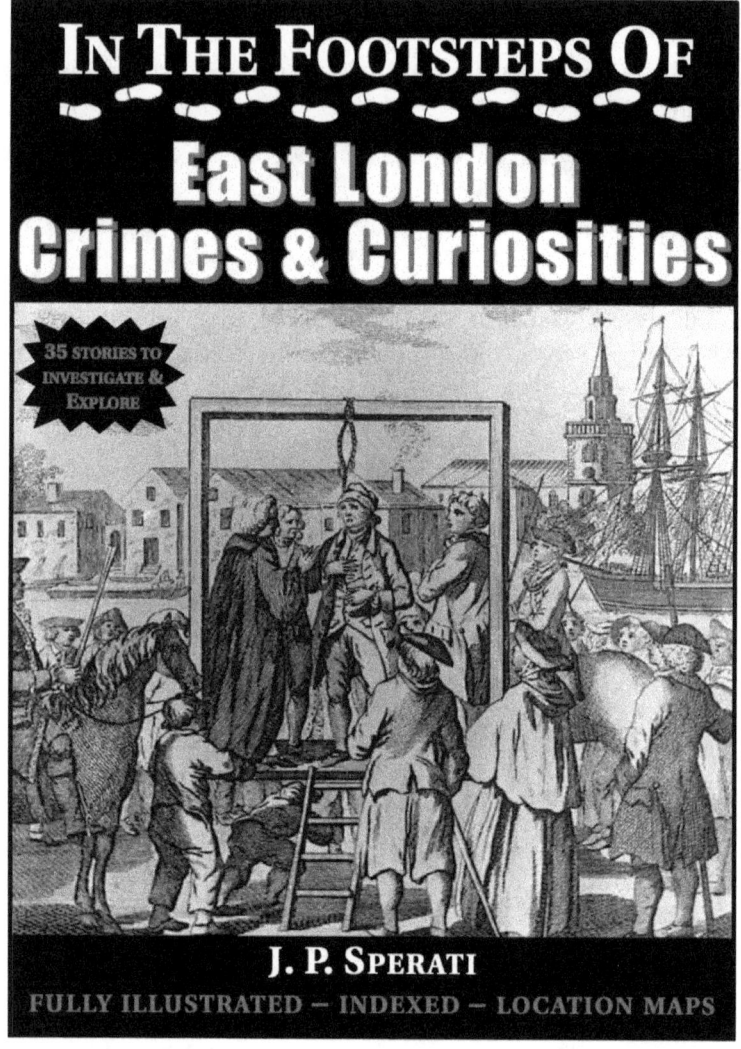

Available in all good bookshops or direct from the publisher at www.crime4u.com

www.ingramcontent.com/pod-product-compliance
Lightning Source LLC
Chambersburg PA
CBHW061641040426
42446CB00010B/1530